THE MESSI
FANBOOK

Eight Ballon d'Or awards. Ten La Liga titles. Four Champions League victories. One Copa América win. Six European Golden Shoes. Two World Cup Golden Balls. Record goalscorer for both Barcelona and Argentina. And finally, in 2022, the greatest prize of them all – one World Cup. The list of Lionel Messi's records, honours and achievements is almost endless, but it also only tells part of his incredible story. In the Lionel Messi Fanbook we look back on how he overcame the odds to become arguably the greatest footballer the world has ever seen. From his early years in Argentina and his reign in Spain to his short spell at PSG, becoming Inter Miami's MVP and winning the World Cup he'd always dreamed of, we relive all the highs and lows from his remarkable career. We also discover his life off the pitch, see how he compares to the greatest players in football history, look back on his top 10 moments, and more! You'll even find four eye-catching and iconic Messi posters inside! Enjoy!

CONTENTS

06
A STAR IS BORN
THE YOUNG GENIUS WITH THE WORLD AT HIS FEET

16
KING OF BARCELONA
FROM SOUTH AMERICAN SUPERKID TO KING OF EUROPE

36
WHO'S THE GOAT?
HOW DOES MESSI STACK UP AGAINST FOOTBALL'S GREATS?

38
THE PSG PROJECT
COULD MESSI BRING EURO GLORY TO PARIS?

47
POSTERS
FOUR LIONEL MESSI A3 PULL-OUT POSTERS

56
TOP 10 MOMENTS
THE HIGHLIGHTS FROM AN INCREDIBLE CAREER

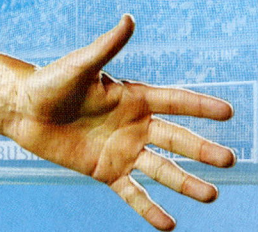

58
THE MIAMI MVP
THE INCREDIBLE JOURNEY CONTINUES STATESIDE

68
ARGENTINA'S NEW MESSIAH
HOW MESSI GOT HIS HANDS ON THE BIGGEST PRIZE

80
MESSI BY NUMBERS
THE KEY NUMBERS FROM MESSI'S CAREER SO FAR

82
OFF THE PITCH
KEEPING BUSY AWAY FROM FOOTBALL

90
RECORD BREAKER
HOW MESSI HAS DOMINATED THE WORLD OF FOOTBALL

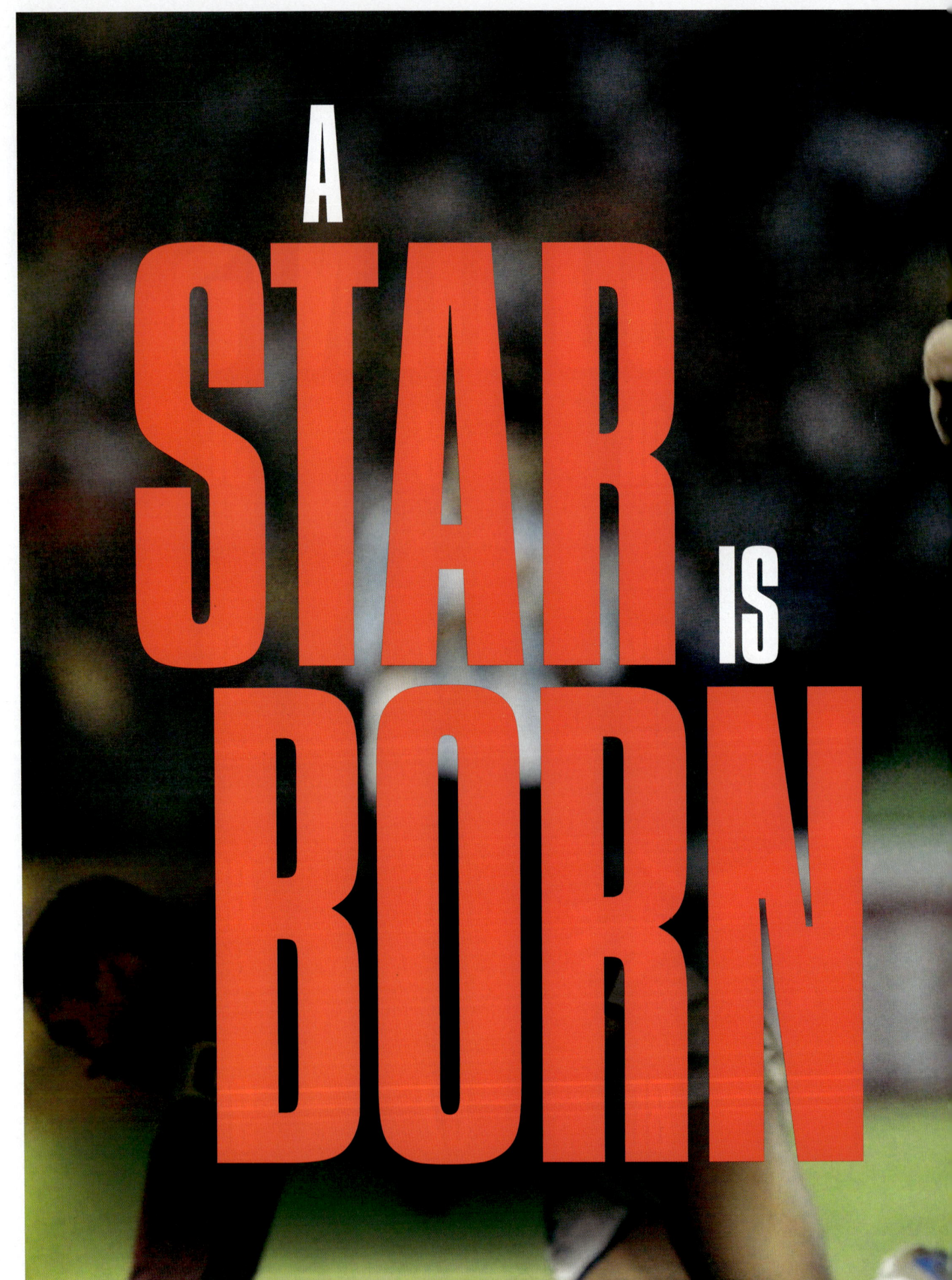

A STAR IS BORN

How a young genius from Rosario with **THE WORLD AT HIS FEET** overcame the odds to become the **HOTTEST PROPERTY ON THE PLANET**

A STAR IS BORN

► **BORN IN JUNE** 1987, Lionel Messi is the third of four children. Young 'Leo' was obsessed with football from an early age, playing with his two elder brothers, Rodrigo and Matías, along with his cousins, Maximiliano and Emanuel Biancucchi. Like Messi, both Maximiliano and Emanuel would go on to become professional footballers, too.

IMAGE: ESCUELA GENERAL LAS HERAS / LATINCONTENT VIA GETTY IMAGES

▼ **THE MESSI FAMILY** lived at 525 Estado de Israel (pictured), in Rosario. His father, Jorge, was a steel factory manager, while his mother, Celia, worked in a magnet manufacturing workshop. Leo himself was of Italian and Spanish descent – and would only live in his native South America until the age of 13, before heading to Catalonia with the whole family to sign for Barcelona.

IMAGE: GABRIEL ROSSI / GETTY IMAGES

A STAR IS BORN

A YOUNG MESSI (second row, third from left) poses for a photo as a student of the first grade at elementary school General Las Heras in Rosario. Messi was said to be an average student as a child – while one of Messi's primary school teachers, Andrea Sosa, noted that he was well-behaved and incredibly shy as a youngster.

IMAGE: ESCUELA GENERAL LAS HERAS / LATINCONTENT VIA GETTY IMAGES

LOPEZ WAS ONE OF THE FIRST TO SEE MESSI'S NATURAL TALENT, AS HE DAZZLED IN 'THE MACHINE OF '87'

MESSI (FRONT, SECOND from the right) joined local club Grandoli when he was four years old, where his first coach was Oscar Lopez. It was Leo's grandmother who first encouraged him in football, with family urging coaches to play him in the age group above. Lopez was one of the first to see Messi's natural talent up close, as he dazzled in 'The Machine of '87', a prolific youth side named after the year of their birth.

IMAGE: ZUMA PRESS, INC. / ALAMY IMAGES

DID YOU KNOW

Messi had several heroes growing up – but perhaps none bigger than Pablo Aimar. Aimar was a typical Argentine No.10, labelled an 'enganche' style of playmaker who rose to prominence at River Plate (who had the chance to sign Messi) before moving to Valencia. Messi was also a huge fan of Brazilian striker Ronaldo, who he would later emulate with his goalscoring exploits. Diego Maradona would also be an influence, with Messi dedicating a goal to his countryman and one-time manager after his death in 2020, by taking off his Barcelona shirt to reveal a Newell's Old Boys shirt with the No.10 on the back (below).

IMAGE: VANDERLEI ALMEIDA / AFP VIA GETTY IMAGES

MESSI JOINED NEWELL'S Old Boys when he was just six years old, scoring an incredible 500 goals in youth football for his boyhood side. He'd be invited, too, to first-team games to perform tricks at half-time for the crowd. The NOB stadium would later be named after legendary Argentine coach Marcelo Bielsa, while the south stand would be named after Diego Maradona – long after Messi departed Rosario for Barcelona.

IMAGE: XINHUA / ALAMY IMAGES

ADRIÁN CORIA IS RECOGNISED as Leo's first true manager and the man who helped hone his skills in Newell's' youth teams before the Messi family upped sticks for Spain. "Generally players either have very good technique and ball control, but they aren't fast," Coria later said of coaching Messi. "Leo was fast and he had brilliant skill, both things together. This made him different."

IMAGE: LUCIANO BISBAL / GETTY IMAGES

⏵
ENDOCRINOLOGIST DIEGO SCHWARZSTEIN diagnosed Leo with a growth hormone deficiency at age ten. Jorge Messi's health insurance only covered two years of treatment: Newell's agreed to contribute, but later reneged on their promise, while one of Argentina's biggest sides, River Plate, refused to pay, too. That left Barcelona in the unusual position of signing a foreign player and committing to his medical treatment in 2001.

IMAGE: CARLOS CARRION / GETTY IMAGES

A STAR IS BORN

CARLES REXACH PLAYED for Barcelona's first team for 17 years, has been coach, assistant coach, technical director and presidential advisor – but perhaps his most important contribution was in signing Messi. After other rejections, Messi's family gave Rexach an ultimatum to sign their son – and the technical secretary responded by hastily writing a contract on a napkin (inset). There have since been calls for it to be placed in the Barcelona museum.

IMAGE: SANDRA BEHNE / BONGARTS / GETTY IMAGES

AFTER OTHER REJECTIONS, MESSI'S FAMILY GAVE CARLES REXACH AN ULTIMATUM TO SIGN THEIR SON

MESSI JOINED THE famed La Masia academy (pictured) in Barcelona in February 2001, aged just 13. Initially, he struggled to settle, unable to play in proper competitions as he was embroiled in a transfer conflict with Newell's: it took a whole year before he was able to play in nationally recognised tournaments, with Messi playing in Catalan competitions and friendlies until then.

IMAGE: JASPER JUINEN / GETTY IMAGES

A STAR IS BORN

MESSI POSES WITH his brother Rodrigo (left), sister María Sol, father Jorge, mother Celia, nephew Tomas and brother Matías (right). Celia and Leo's siblings returned to Argentina over the summer of 2001: with Leo at a crossroads and Jorge not yet paid by Barcelona, the family considered all moving back together. Messi insisted on staying, however, determined to succeed at the Camp Nou. He was rewarded in December of that year with a new contract.
IMAGE: MARCELO BOERI/EL GRAFICO / GETTY IMAGES

SPAIN WERE DESPERATE to secure Messi for the national team, with Rexach alerting the Spanish setup that Leo was eligible for La Roja. The Argentine Football Association were so desperate themselves to tie their player down, however, they organised two under-20 friendlies in June 2004, to finalise his FIFA status. They needn't have worried: Messi had always dreamed of representing Argentina over Spain.
IMAGE: JORGE DOMINELLI/EL GRAFICO / GETTY IMAGES

MESSI WAS QUIET and unassuming when he first began at Barcelona, referred to as 'the mute' by other boys because he got changed in silence and let his football do the talking. In barely a year and a half of playing teenage football in Catalonia though, he moved up five youth levels, scoring bucketloads at every one. During his first full season, he was top scorer with 36 goals in 30 games.

IMAGE: MARCELO BOERI / EL GRAFICO / GETTY IMAGES

A STAR IS BORN

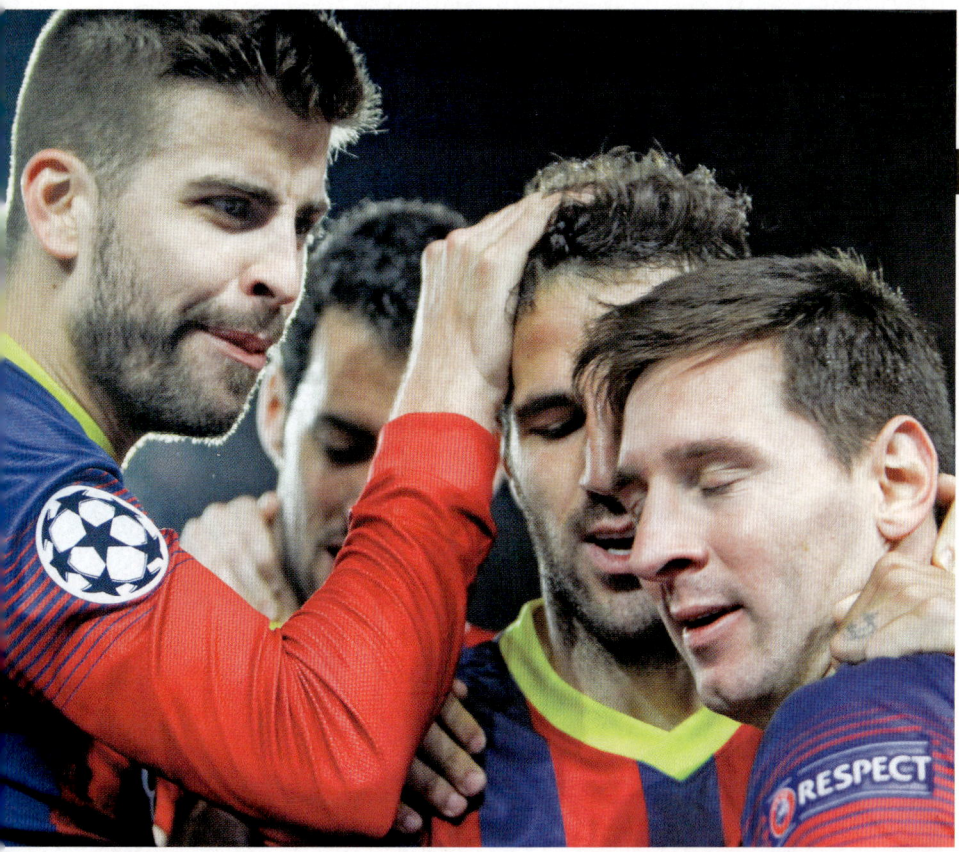

> **MESSI WOULD BECOME** close with the likes of Gerard Piqué (left) and Cesc Fàbregas (next to Messi), tearing opponents apart in Barcelona's 'Baby Dream Team' at youth level. While the trio would be reunited at Barça years later, Piqué would leave for Manchester United, while Fàbregas would go to Arsenal. Gunners boss Arsène Wenger wanted to take all three Barcelona talents, believing Messi would become the greatest of them all. Arsenal were Messi's first offer from a foreign club – but he stayed loyal to Barça.
> IMAGE: NURPHOTO / GETTY IMAGES

MESSI WAS QUIET AND UNASSUMING WHEN HE STARTED AT BARÇA… HE GOT CHANGED IN SILENCE AND LET HIS FOOTBALL DO THE TALKING

> **IN 2003, BARCELONA** manager Frank Rijkaard brought Messi off the bench in a friendly against José Mourinho's Porto for his very first taste of first-team action in a Blaugrana shirt, alongside the likes of Luis Enrique and Xavi. "He is a boy with a lot of talent," the Dutch manager would say of young Leo's first cameo.
> IMAGE: LLUIS GENE / GETTY IMAGES

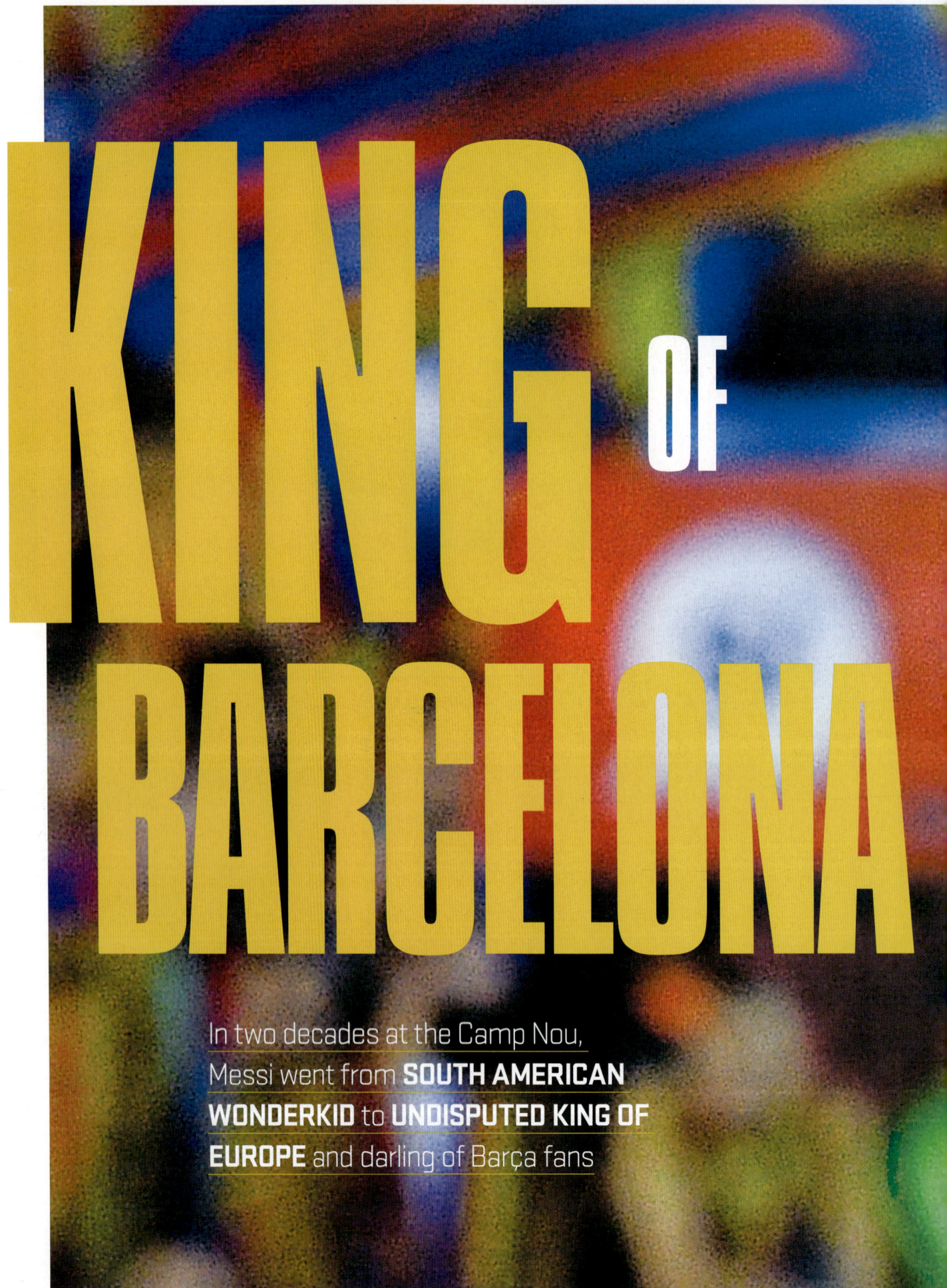

KING OF BARCELONA

In two decades at the Camp Nou, Messi went from **SOUTH AMERICAN WONDERKID** to **UNDISPUTED KING OF EUROPE** and darling of Barça fans

KING OF BARCELONA

LIONEL MESSI BURST onto the scene in 2005 with a goal off the bench against Albacete to become Barcelona's youngest-ever scorer. In celebration, Ronaldinho gave a piggyback to the boy he labelled his "little brother" in the team. When Ronaldinho was later asked if he was the best player in the world, the Brazilian responded, "I'm not even the best at Barça," referring to the talented teenager who would usurp him at Camp Nou and take his No.10 shirt to boot.

IMAGE: LLUIS GENE / AFP VIA GETTY IMAGES

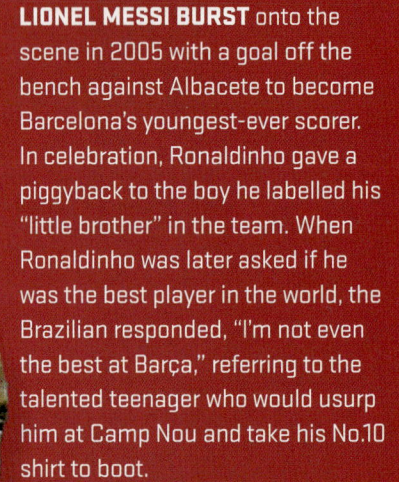

IN 2007 MESSI LAID DOWN A MARKER ON THE BIGGEST STAGE, RECORDING HIS FIRST-EVER SENIOR HAT-TRICK AGAINST RIVALS REAL MADRID

AT STAMFORD BRIDGE in the Champions League in 2006, Messi began to show the rest of Europe what he was capable of. Chelsea players did their best to try and rough up the young Argentine winger, who was just too quick and too skilful for the Blues defence. Messi stunned José Mourinho's team – and not for the last time. Barça would go on to win the Champions League that season, with Messi playing a modest role.

IMAGE: MIKE HEWITT / GETTY IMAGES

KING OF BARCELONA

▸ **IN MARCH 2007** Messi laid down a marker on the biggest stage of all. The little genius recorded his first-ever senior hat-trick against Barcelona's bitter rivals Real Madrid, as the youngster equalised three times to earn his side a point in El Clásico. Messi eventually left Barça with 26 goals in one of club football's biggest fixtures: more than anyone else and eight ahead of Cristiano Ronaldo in second place.

IMAGE: CESAR RANGEL / AFP VIA GETTY IMAGES

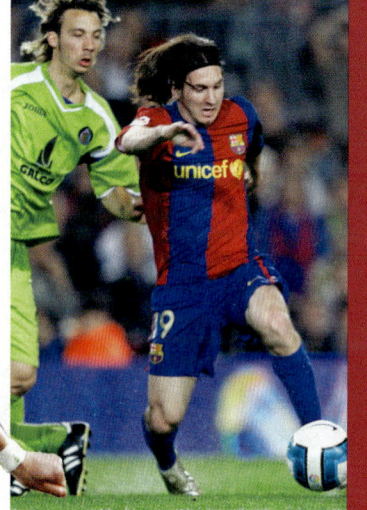

◂ **JUST A FEW** weeks later Messi scored arguably the greatest goal of all time during the Copa del Rey semi-final. Picking up possession on the halfway line at the Camp Nou, he ghosted past an ever-gathering chorus of Getafe defenders and danced towards goal before rounding the keeper and slotting home a stunning goal reminiscent of Diego Maradona's 'Goal of the Century'. Barça won the game 5-2... only to lose the second leg 4-0.

IMAGE: LLUIS GENE / AFP VIA GETTY IMAGES

◂ **SO FEW WOULD** ever compete on the same plane as Messi – but one would get closer than most. In 2008, Cristiano Ronaldo's Manchester United would defeat Leo's Barça in the semi-finals en route to their third Champions League, establishing the young Portuguese player as one of the best on the planet. A gauntlet had been thrown down to the Argentine to match the same heights – and the pair's rivalry would become one of the greatest sport had ever witnessed.

IMAGE: JASPER JUINEN / GETTY IMAGES

DID YOU KNOW

Messi's career could have worked out very differently – if Barcelona president Joan Laporta had accepted a world-record bid for him in 2006. The Barça chief claimed that Italian giants Inter Milan tabled a £225 million offer for the Argentine, some four times the record for a footballer at the time. Had Messi moved, not only would he have never played under Pep Guardiola, but Barcelona may never have won those four Champions League titles. And what of Inter with Messi? Well hiring former Barcelona coach José Mourinho in 2010 would have given the Portuguese the chance to work with the little genius after all. Football could have looked very different…

IMAGE: JOSEP LAGO / GETTY IMAGES

IN 2008, AFTER sacking manager Frank Rijkaard, Barcelona were given a stark choice between Pep Guardiola and José Mourinho as possible replacements. Both had roots at the club, though Mourinho had serial trophy-winning experience. Instead, Barça opted for Guardiola: in his first summer, he jettisoned Deco and Ronaldinho, and fought his bosses to allow Messi to go to the Olympics in Beijing – as he had done in 1992. It was a masterstroke, as Messi flourished in his first few months under Pep.

IMAGE: LLUIS GENE / GETTY IMAGES

KING OF BARCELONA

GUARDIOLA'S FAMED 'TIKI-TAKA' TRANSFORMED FOOTBALL, WITH MESSI THE JEWEL IN HIS CROWN

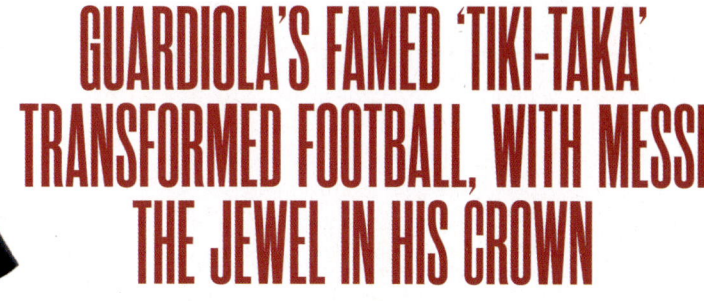

PEP GUARDIOLA'S BARCELONA would cap off an extraordinary season with a Treble, culminating in the club's third Champions League title in 2009 after lifting a La Liga title and Copa del Rey. Messi was the headline-maker in the final against Manchester United, heading Barça's second goal and securing the trophy. Guardiola's famed 'tiki-taka' transformed football, introducing new principles and sweeping across Europe, with Messi the jewel in his crown.

IMAGE: FILIPPO MONTEFORTE / GETTY IMAGES

KING OF BARCELONA

WINNING THREE TROPHIES wasn't enough for Messi and his teammates – they also lifted the Supercopa de Espana, Super Cup and the Club World Cup in Abu Dhabi against Estudiantes of Messi's native Argentina to complete a sumptuous sextuple in 2009. Naturally, the No.10 struck the sucker punch ten minutes away from penalties in extra time of the Club World Cup final. For the first time, Messi and Barcelona were champions of the world.

IMAGE: JASPER JUINEN / GETTY IMAGES

WINNING THREE TROPHIES WASN'T ENOUGH FOR MESSI AND HIS TEAMMATES

FRENCH NEWSPAPER, *L'EQUIPE*, is famously stingy when it comes to awarding ten-out-of-ten performances but even it took a bow when Messi hit Arsenal for four in the 2010 Champions League, tearing apart the north Londoners with ease, scoring a sublime first-half hat-trick before rounding the game off late on. "He's like a PlayStation," Gunners boss Arsene Wenger would exclaim in the aftermath: but Barça would lose in the semi-final to eventual winners, Inter Milan.

IMAGE: JASPER JUINEN / AFP VIA GETTY IMAGES

KING OF BARCELONA

MOURINHO ARRIVED AT Barcelona's bitter rivals Real Madrid in 2010, pitting the two greatest minds of a generation – and the two greatest players – against one another. November's Clásico was one of the most shocking scorelines in the fixture's history, however, with Barça romping home 5-0 winners. Once again, Messi was central, dovetailing with his fellow forwards in one of the all-time great games between the two sides.

IMAGE: JASPER JUINEN / GETTY IMAGES

THE SPANISH GIANTS would renew their rivalry in a Champions League semi-final El Clásico in 2011. In another enthralling instalment between the sides, Barça would triumph 3-1 on aggregate, with Messi supplying the godlike genius once more. He would score the pick of the goals in a heated first leg, picking the ball up from Sergio Busquets in midfield and driving 30 yards towards goal before finding the back of the net and silencing the Bernabéu.

IMAGE: ALEX LIVESEY / AFP VIA GETTY IMAGES

KING OF BARCELONA

MESSI'S THIRD CHAMPIONS League title came, once again, at the expense of Manchester United, this time at Wembley in 2011. While Messi popped up with the winner in 2009, he was the heartbeat of this victory, putting in one of the all-time European final displays to destroy the Red Devils without so much as breaking a sweat. Losing manager Sir Alex Ferguson would call this the greatest side he'd ever face: few would disagree with him.

IMAGE: JASPER JUINEN / AFP VIA GETTY IMAGES

AT 24 YEARS old, Messi stepped into the hallowed annals of Barcelona history, netting a hat-trick to break the Catalan side's all-time scoring record of 232 goals in all competitions. It was just one of several records that the Argentine would break that year – overtaking a 57-year record that was previously held by César Rodríguez.

IMAGE: ALEX CAPARROS / GETTY IMAGES

ON ANOTHER EXCEPTIONAL night in the Champions League, Messi scored five against Bayer Leverkusen, in a performance that perhaps managed to top anything that even he had done. "The only credit I can take is that I always put him in the team and we just try to make sure he gets the ball. After that our task is done," Guardiola gushed post-match. "The throne belongs to him and only he will decide when he wants to relinquish it."

IMAGE: LLUIS GENE / AFP VIA GETTY IMAGES

IN 2012, MESSI would score a simply astounding 91 goals in a calendar year for club and country, with 79 of those strikes coming for Barcelona. The haul beat a 40-year record of 85 goals held by Bayern Munich and Germany's Gerd Müller. The 2011-12 season also saw Messi plunder a staggering 50 goals in La Liga, 14 in the Champions League and 73 in 60 appearances in all competitions. In the following season, Messi scored 60 goals in all competitions with 46 coming in La Liga as Barcelona were once again crowned Spanish champions under new head coach Tito Vilanova.

IMAGE: JASPER JUINEN / AFP VIA GETTY IMAGES

IN NOVEMBER 2014, Messi broke the record for number of goals in La Liga, surpassing Telmo Zarra's 251 goals to net his 252nd in the Spanish top flight in a 5-1 win over Sevilla. It's scarcely believable but the Argentine would go on to almost double that incredible haul during the remainder of his career in Spain, recording 474 strikes before leaving the country in 2021, ahead of Ronaldo on 311.

IMAGE: DAVID RAMOS / GETTY IMAGES

ANOTHER CHAMPIONS LEAGUE victory, another iconic moment in a semi-final. En route to yet another European title in 2015, Barcelona beat former mentor Guardiola's Bayern Munich, with Messi sitting German defender Jérôme Boateng down at Camp Nou before netting. Barça would sweep another Treble, this time under Luis Enrique, who played in Messi's first-ever first team appearance against Porto.

IMAGE: VLADIMIR RYS PHOTOGRAPHY / GETTY IMAGES

KING OF BARCELONA

IN THE COPA del Rey final in 2015, Messi would score yet another solo wonder goal, dubbed the 'impossible goal'. Picking the ball up on the touchline close to the halfway line, Messi slalomed through three Athletic Bilbao defenders, beating them as they converged on him before whipping the ball past goalkeeper Iago Herrerín at his near post to give Barcelona the lead. The goal came second in the Puskás Award of that year.

IMAGE: DAVID RAMOS / GETTY IMAGES

THE SOUTH AMERICAN TRIO RACKED UP A FRIGHTENING 364 GOALS IN 450 APPEARANCES

IN 2016, MESSI recorded his 500th senior goal against Valencia, alongside Luis Suárez and Neymar in the famed 'MSN' frontline. The South American trio racked up a frightening 364 goals in 450 appearances together, with Messi claiming 153 of those alone. The attacking triumvirate has become renowned as one of the most ferocious in footballing history, with the three players said to be friends off the field, too.

IMAGE: MATTHIAS HANGST / GETTY IMAGES

KING OF BARCELONA

THE IMPOSSIBLE UNFOLDED in 2017, when Barcelona became the first team in history to overturn a four-goal deficit to progress in a Champions League knockout tie. After a 4-0 thrashing in Paris in the first leg, Messi and co produced a remarkable comeback to beat PSG 6-1 at home and progress to the quarter-finals. While Messi wasn't the central protagonist this time, the game had a huge impact on his career: Neymar decided to step out of the Argentine's shadow and depart in a world-record €222 million transfer – to Paris Saint-Germain, of all clubs – at the end of the season.

IMAGE: LAURENCE GRIFFITHS / GETTY IMAGES

IN APRIL 2017, Real Madrid and Barcelona put on one of the most beloved Clásico contests ever witnessed. Los Blancos took the lead before Messi got Barça back on level terms; Ivan Rakitić then put Barcelona ahead before James Rodríguez equalised. The game was heading for a stalemate, however, in injury time, Messi finished an exquisite move and a pulsating contest, racing to the crowd to hold his No.10 jersey aloft. Absolutely iconic.

IMAGE: SIPA US / ALAMY STOCK PHOTO

▲ **WHILE MESSI WAS** still lauded as the greatest on Earth, Barcelona were no longer afforded such lofty praise. The first of three humiliations came in 2018, when Roma 'rose from their ruins' to stun Barça with a 'remontada' of their own, overturning a 4-1 Camp Nou defeat to beat Messi's side 3-0 in the Eternal City and progress on away goals – a nightmare night for Catalan colours.

IMAGE: ANDREAS SOLARO / GETTY IMAGES

MESSI FINISHED AN EXQUISITE MOVE AND A PULSATING CONTEST

▶ **ANDRÉS INIESTA'S DEPARTURE** in the summer of 2018 left a captaincy void – which would be filled by the boy who was once thought too quiet to be a leader. Messi assumed the captain's armband, leading the Blaugrana to a Supercoppa as his first trophy and proving himself to be a worthy captain of a different kind: quiet, sure, but stoic and strong, leading in his actions rather than his words.

IMAGE: FADEL SENNA / GETTY IMAGES

KING OF BARCELONA

AFTER SCORING A beautiful free-kick past Alisson Becker at the Camp Nou in the Champions League semi-finals of 2019, Liverpool – minus Mohamed Salah and Sadio Mané – were the second side in two years to wipe the smile off Messi's face with an unbelievable comeback in the return leg. The Reds smashed Barcelona 4-0 at Anfield, with Messi cutting a lonely figure in the end: this super team were truly mortal after all.

IMAGE: SHAUN BOTTERILL / GETTY IMAGES

KING OF BARCELONA

DID YOU KNOW

The teammate that Messi shared the pitch with most times? That would be Sergio Busquets (below). Barcelona would field the pair during 567 games (they would also link up again at Inter Miami), with Busquets assuming the captaincy after Messi departed for the US. Gerard Piqué was second on the list, with Andrés Iniesta third. And Messi's most-faced opponent? Well, Cristiano Ronaldo is only fourth on the list, with Diego Godín and Karim Benzema second and third respectively. It was Real Madrid's ferocious captain Sergio Ramos who played against Messi most often. Of course, the two players would become teammates in Paris...

IMAGE: SOCCRATES IMAGES / GETTY IMAGES

MESSI CUT A LONELY FIGURE — THIS SUPER TEAM WERE TRULY MORTAL

THOUGH EUROPEAN GLORY evaded Messi in the latter years of his Camp Nou career, records continued to tumble. A tenth La Liga title and record sixth Pichichi Trophy as the league's top scorer eased the blow of the Liverpool defeat, with a sixth Golden Shoe award following. That was a record third consecutive time Messi had been Europe's top scorer.

IMAGE: PAU BARRENA / GETTY IMAGES

KING OF BARCELONA

▼ **THINGS WERE TO** get worse for Messi and Barcelona in the Champions League in 2020. Behind closed doors in a single-legged quarter-final match during the COVID lockdown, Bayern Munich obliterated Barcelona 8-2. The match was to be Suárez's last, among others, as Messi contemplated his future at a financially wrecked Barça and sought pastures new. Manchester City were said to be interested – though ultimately, the Argentine was denied his move.

IMAGE: MANU FERNANDEZ / GETTY IMAGES

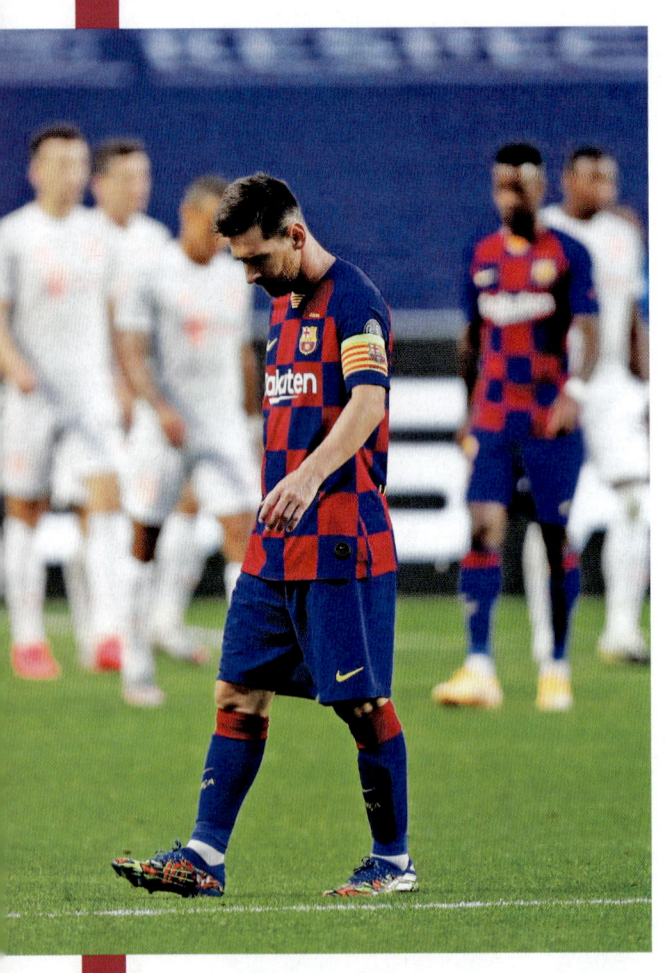

▶ **IN DECEMBER 2020**, Messi broke Pelé's record of the most goals for one club, after scoring his 644th goal for Barcelona during a win over Real Valladolid. A year later, he lifted the Copa del Rey, his last piece of silverware in a Barcelona shirt. It was time for him to leave Catalonia, having scored a staggering 672 times in 778 appearances.

IMAGE: FRAN SANTIAGO / GETTY IMAGES

KING OF BARCELONA

IN A TEARY PRESS CONFERENCE, MESSI BID FAREWELL TO THE CITY AND THE CLUB THAT HE'D SERVED FOR 20 YEARS

▼ **BARCELONA WANTED TO** keep Messi – and Messi had since changed his stance and committed to a new deal. But La Liga wouldn't allow the signing, given that Barça were well over their wage budget. In a teary press conference, Messi addressed his teammates and bid farewell to the city and the club that he'd served for 20 years. Messi won 35 major trophies with Barcelona, leaving their most decorated player ever.

IMAGE: ERIC ALONSO / GETTY IMAGES

WHO'S THE GOAT?

Messi is arguably the **GREATEST PLAYER TO HAVE EVER LIVED** – but how does he compare to other footballing legends?

PELÉ

YEARS ACTIVE 1956-77
NATIONALITY Brazilian
MAJOR HONOURS 3x World Cups, 5x Brazilian Serie As, 2x Copa Libertadores

- The first true superstar of football, Pelé invented plenty, scored loads and is still the only man to have ever won three World Cups. He became an icon in Brazil, helping to establish the nation as football's spiritual entertainers, as well as a hotbed for samba-infused street talent: it's because of him that the No.10 has any kind of prestige, too.

ZINEDINE ZIDANE

YEARS ACTIVE 1989-2006
NATIONALITY French
MAJOR HONOURS 1x World Cup, 1x European Championship, 1x Champions League, 1x La Liga, 2x Serie As, 1x Ballon d'Or

- The most majestic midfielder of his era, Zinedine Zidane had a velvet touch and a fire within him. The Frenchman was a big-game player who netted two in a World Cup final in Paris, one of the greatest Champions League-winning goals ever and finished his career with a red card for a headbutt. Everything in between was sumptuous.

RONALDO

YEARS ACTIVE 1993-2011
NATIONALITY Brazilian
MAJOR HONOURS 2x World Cups, 2x Copa Américas, 1x UEFA Cup, 1x La Liga, 2x Ballons d'Or

- The complete forward when he burst onto the scene, Ronaldo Nazario was an unplayable alien who raised the bar on what so many thought possible from a modern forward. Injury would plague him and rob him of longevity but in terms of his absolute peak, we may never see such a pure distillation of brilliance than late-90s, original Ronaldo.

DIEGO MARADONA

YEARS ACTIVE 1976-97
NATIONALITY Argentinian
MAJOR HONOURS 1x World Cup, 2x Serie As, 1x UEFA Cup

- Maverick, madman, Maradona: Diego was the most controversial, most ingenious footballer of his time, capable of the brilliant and the insane all at once. A master of dribbling, a lethal set-piece king and a tricky one-man whirlwind who could turn defenders inside out, he was best when he was dragging his teams to trophies. A huge influence for Messi.

JOHAN CRUYFF

YEARS ACTIVE 1964-84
NATIONALITY Dutch
MAJOR HONOURS 9x Eredivisies, 3x European Cups, 1x La Liga, 3x Ballons d'Or

- Tall, rake-like, with a Beatles haircut, Johan Cruyff was football's greatest artist and the picture postcard of Total Football. The fulcrum of the Dutch side that invented the game's greatest philosophy, Cruyff himself was an innovator, a rebel and a supremely talented and intelligent individual. His influence as a coach was unmatched, too.

GEORGE BEST

YEARS ACTIVE 1963-83
NATIONALITY Northern Irish
MAJOR HONOURS 1x European Cup, 2x English First Divisions, 1x Ballon d'Or

- The first playboy footballer, George Best was as beguiling off the pitch as he was on it. A mazy dribbler of sheer technical excellence, the Northern Irishman was the flair of Manchester United's Holy Trinity alongside Bobby Charlton and Denis Law, redefining British football for a generation and making celebrities of humble sportsmen. He burned bright, all right.

FRANZ BECKENBAUER

YEARS ACTIVE 1964-83
NATIONALITY German
MAJOR HONOURS 3x European Cups, 5x Bundesligas, 1x World Cup, 1x European Championship, 2x Ballons d'Or

- Regarded as one of the best defenders of all time, Franz Beckenbauer is the model German player and thought of as the country's footballing father. Der Kaiser was on the losing side in 1966's World Cup final but rarely again after that, becoming a presence at the back, a figure of wisdom and experience, and winning everything in the game.

LIONEL MESSI

YEARS ACTIVE 2003-present
NATIONALITY Argentinian
MAJOR HONOURS 1x World Cup, 1x Copa América, 4x Champions Leagues, 10x La Ligas, 8x Ballons d'Or

- Perhaps the best dribbler, passer and ball-striker of a generation, Messi changed the sport forever, elevating statistical output from forwards and moving the game into a realm of diminutive attackers who used brain as much as brawn. He's been at the forefront of the modern game and is as celebrated for his beauty on the ball as much as his efficiency.

CRISTIANO RONALDO

YEARS ACTIVE 2002-present
NATIONALITY Portuguese
MAJOR HONOURS 5x Champions Leagues, 1x European Championship, 3x Premier Leagues, 2x La Ligas, 5x Ballons d'Or

- No one has ever been a better example for the power of mentality. Cristiano Ronaldo began his career as a showpony-like winger, before evolving into a ferocious goalscorer, a man for big occasions and football's most expensive player, for a while. His rivalry with Messi pitted the pair on opposite sides of the El Clásico divide and as contrasting philosophies.

ALFREDO DI STEFANO

YEARS ACTIVE 1945-66
NATIONALITY Argentinian
MAJOR HONOURS 5x European Cups, 8x La Ligas, 1x Copa América, 2x Ballons d'Or

- The European Cup's first true hero, Alfredo Di Stefano was Real Madrid's A-lister in the 1950s and one of the finest to have ever played the game. His trophy haul is still almost unmatched – as is his influence as a classy, dominant forward who defined the Los Blancos institution in the glory days.

THE PSG

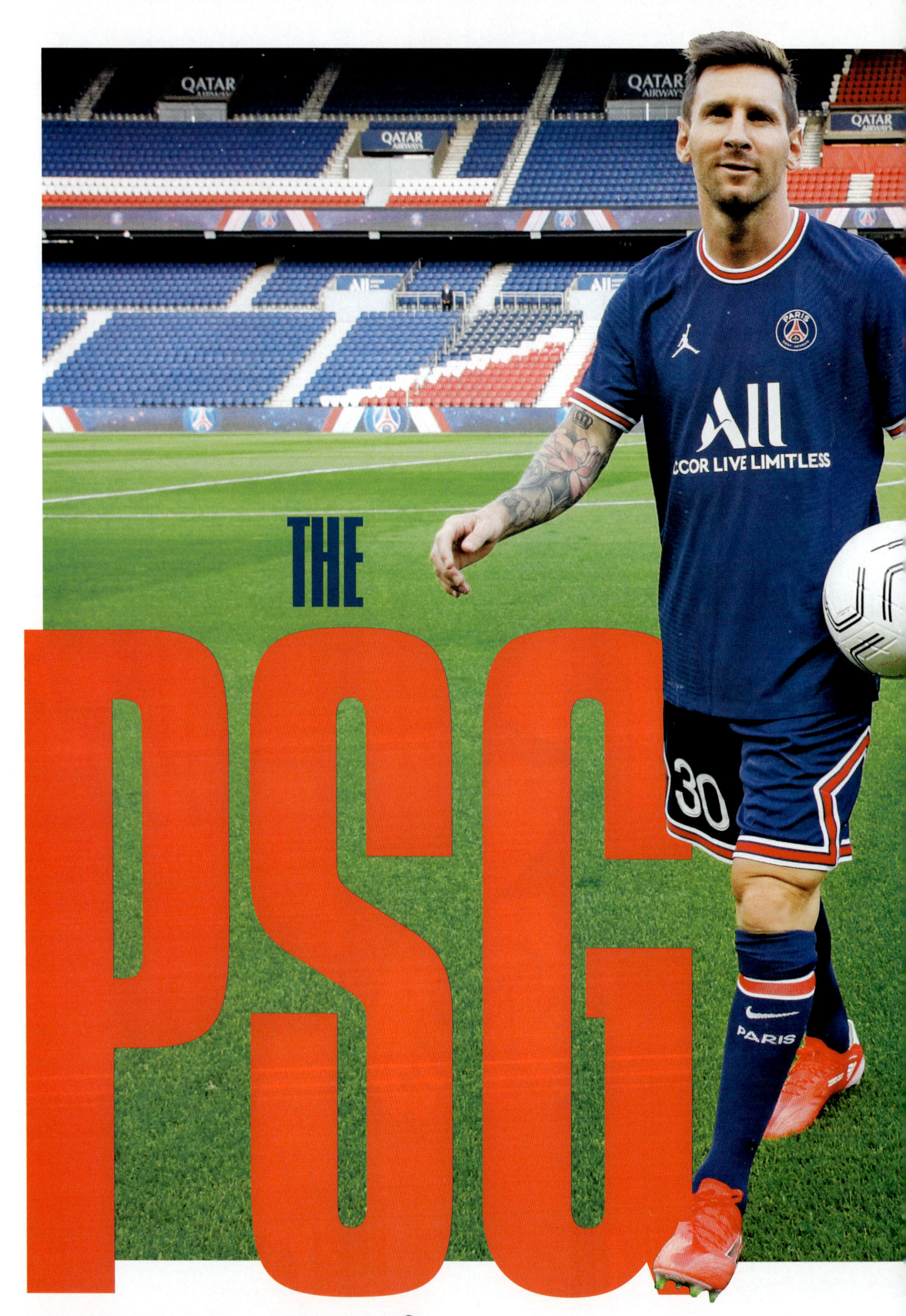

PROJECT

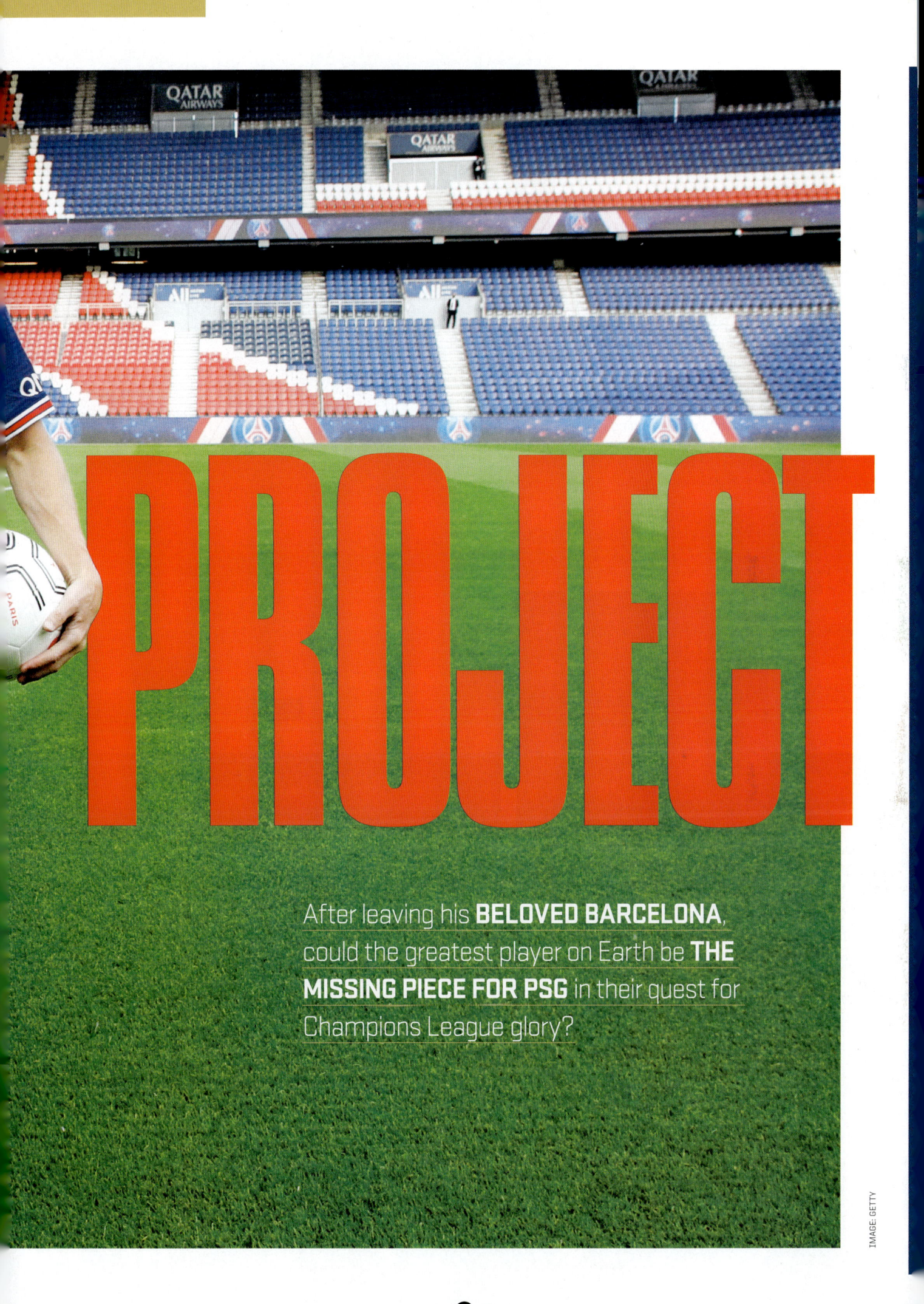

After leaving his **BELOVED BARCELONA**, could the greatest player on Earth be **THE MISSING PIECE FOR PSG** in their quest for Champions League glory?

THE PSG PROJECT

▶ **FOLLOWING HIS TEARFUL** exit from Barcelona in 2021, Messi moved to another huge European city building their own project of world-beating stars. The Argentine moved to Paris on a free transfer, shocking the world as he penned a two-year deal with the option of another year. As he posed at the Parc des Princes, it was clear: this was a superstar even PSG hadn't dared to dream signing.

IMAGE: PARIS SAINT-GERMAIN FOOTBALL / PSG VIA GETTY IMAGES

▼ **IT WAS A** frontline to rival not just any in the world – but any in history. Messi rekindled his spark with Neymar from his Barcelona days to pick up where they left off, while Kylian Mbappé, the next great Galáctico of the game, completed the lineup. Messi was given more of a creative role to supply the young Frenchman. This was Mbappé's backyard: something Leo wasn't used to.

IMAGE: JAN KRUGER - UEFA / UEFA VIA GETTY IMAGES

IT WAS A FRONTLINE TO RIVAL NOT JUST ANY IN THE WORLD — BUT ANY IN HISTORY

THE PSG PROJECT

MESSI'S PARIS SAINT-GERMAIN debut came off the bench away to Stade De Reims in August 2021, fittingly, replacing former Barça teammate Neymar. Though he'd left La Liga, however, Messi's bow in French football averaged over two million viewers in Spain, making it the most-watched Ligue 1 football game in the country ever. Mbappé scored both goals on the night.

IMAGE: JOHN BERRY / GETTY IMAGES

NEW COLOURS, FAMILIAR foe... same result. Messi's first goal in the blue of PSG came against former mentor Pep Guardiola and Manchester City, with the two oil-rich giants of European football pitted against one another in the Champions League group stage. The clashes between the two clubs were like chess matches, with endless technical quality on either side.

IMAGE: CATHERINE STEENKESTE / GETTY IMAGES

WHILE GOALS WERE a little harder to come by than at Barcelona, Messi's influence in Paris was still felt. He racked up three assists away to Saint-Etienne – the fifth time he'd managed a hat-trick of assists in his career – in a virtuoso performance that beautifully summed up his creative abilities. Only 15 games had been played in the season – and PSG were already 12 points clear and running away with the league.

IMAGE: MARCIO MACHADO / GETTY IMAGES

THE PSG PROJECT

PSG WERE FINALLY STARTING TO LOOK LIKE THE REAL DEAL

PSG BEAT REAL Madrid 1-0 at home in the last-16 of the Champions League in February 2022, with Mbappé delivering the killer blow late on in the game. Messi may have missed a penalty but this side were finally starting to look like the real deal after years of underwhelming performances under the bright lights of European football.

IMAGE: AURELIEN MEUNIER - PSG/ PSG VIA GETTY IMAGES

THE PSG PROJECT

> **THIS CHAMPIONS LEAGUE** tie was firmly in Parisien hands. PSG were electric at times in the second leg at the Bernabéu, as Mbappé put the French side 2-0 up on aggregate – and they were cruising into the quarter-finals with just half an hour remaining. That was, until, the impossible. Karim Benzema hit a dramatic hat-trick to sink Messi and co, sending them crashing out of the competition. It was the kind of thing we'd seen so often from the Argentine himself.
>
> IMAGE: DIEGO SOUTO / QUALITY SPORT IMAGES / GETTY IMAGES

> **BOOED BY A** section of the Parc des Princes at home to Bordeaux after elimination in Europe, the honeymoon was well and truly over for Messi. Some PSG fans became impatient for long-coveted success in the Champions League, now that they had one of the greatest players ever, with manager Mauricio Pochettino forced to defend his superstars.
>
> IMAGE: TIM CLAYTON / CORBIS VIA GETTY IMAGES

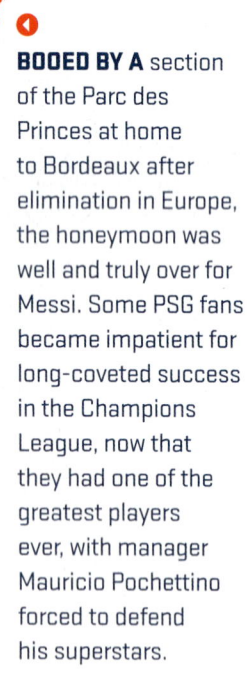

THE PSG PROJECT

THANKS IN PART to a Messi thunderbolt, PSG were champions against Lens in the Argentine's first season outside Spain. It felt like an underwhelming season, however: Messi's debut season finished with 11 goals and 14 assists across all competitions but with just six in the league, it was his lowest return since 2006. Mauricio Pochettino, among others, would leave, as PSG looked to strengthen.

IMAGE: JEAN CATUFFE / GETTY IMAGES

DID YOU KNOW

Messi was arguably the most famous No.10 in the world – but he found that when he arrived in Paris, the iconic shirt number was already held by former teammate Neymar. Feeling it was a little rude to ask for his favoured jersey, Messi reflected on new beginnings and went for a nostalgic option for his shirt number, choosing the No.30. This was the number he wore after breaking into the first team at Barcelona: intriguingly though, the No.30 was previously only allowed to be worn by goalkeepers in Ligue 1 – making Messi one of the first outfield players to don the digit in France.

IMAGE: TIM CLAYTON / CORBIS VIA GETTY IMAGES

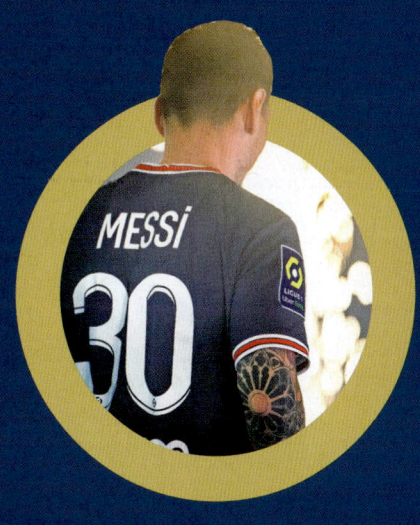

MESSI BEGAN TO enjoy his football once more in his second season. Deployed in a more fluid role in the attack, he began dictating play a lot more, winning the Ligue 1 Player of the Month in September 2022 and scoring against Benfica to clock up 40 different Champions League opponents that he'd netted against. It took just 18 matches to equal his goal output from the previous campaign.

IMAGE: JOSE BRETON / PICS ACTION / NURPHOTO VIA GETTY IMAGES

THE PSG PROJECT

▶ **IN FEBRUARY 2023**, PSG raced into a 2-0 lead against Lille, before being pegged back to 3-3. Of course: Messi would score the winner from a free kick in the dying minutes in one of the last moments of pure bedlam he'd cause in European football. That month he'd score his 700th senior career club goal; weeks later, he'd rack up his 300th club career assist. The records kept tumbling.

IMAGE: TIM CLAYTON/CORBIS VIA GETTY IMAGES

▶ **PARIS SAINT-GERMAIN'S WAIT** for European glory couldn't be ended by one man. Once again, the French giants were beaten in the first knockout round, this time by a brilliant Bayern Munich across two legs, with Messi somewhat anonymous in the tie. And he wasn't the only one: the PSG project was starting to feel a little stale, with the huge investment failing to deliver the biggest prize of all. A reset was due.

IMAGE: CHRIS BRUNSKILL / FANTASISTA / GETTY IMAGES

▶ **ONE LAST DANCE?** Messi and Ronaldo would face each other in a scheduled friendly, with PSG travelling out to Saudi Arabia – but Messi would later find himself in hot water with his employers over an undisclosed trip to the Gulf State. Messi missed training, invoking the fury of fans who already felt he was disconnected from the club. He apologised – but the writing was already on the wall.

IMAGE: FRANCK FIFE / AFP VIA GETTY IMAGES

CATCH ME IF YOU CAN
Messi takes on the entire
Atletico Madrid defence during
the Copa del Rey semi-final
second leg in February 2017

ALL HAIL THE KING
Messi celebrates in front of the Argentina fans after scoring a vital goal against Mexico at the 2022 World Cup

TOP OF THE WORLD
Messi emulates his hero
Diego Maradona after
lifting the World Cup for
Argentina in 2022

THE MIAMI MVP
Messi celebrates after scoring for Inter Miami against Atlanta United during their Leagues Cup match in July 2023

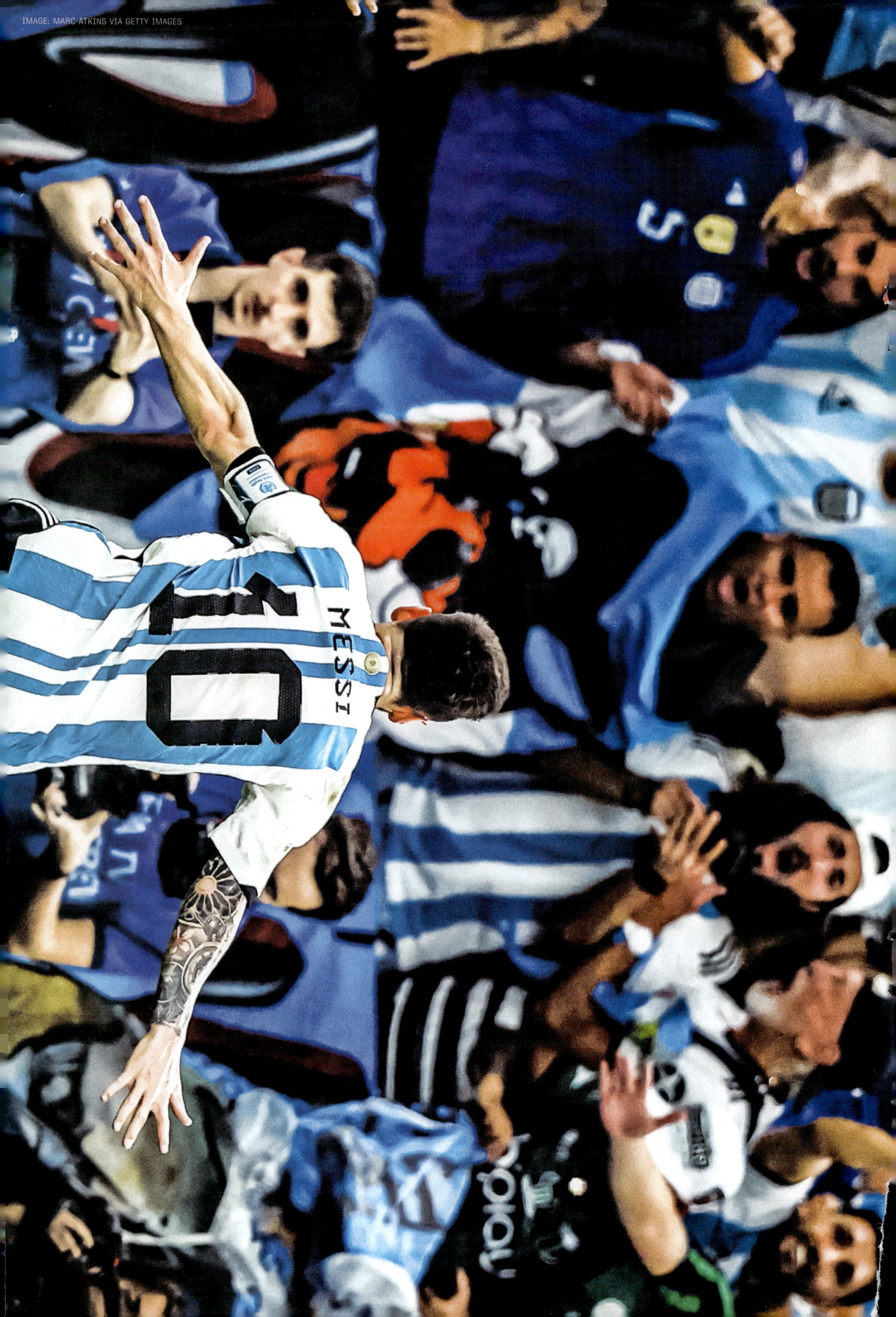

IMAGE: MARC ATKINS VIA GETTY IMAGES

IMAGE: ALEX CAPARROS / STRINGER VIA GETTY IMAGES

▶ **AFTER TWO YEARS**, Messi's contract was not renewed at PSG: the signing had not been seen as a success. Les Parisiens' insatiable thirst for a European title had led them to secure the biggest star in the history of the sport – but despite two French titles, last-16 Champions League exits had left them feeling disenchanted. The club was set for a rebuild – and Messi managed to part amicably with the majority of supporters.

IMAGE: MUSTAFA YALCIN / ANADOLU AGENCY VIA GETTY IMAGES

MESSI'S TOP 10 MOMENTS

Amid a galaxy of star-studded moments, these are the highlights from **ONE OF THE GREATEST** careers in football history

ON TOP OF THE WORLD
18 December 2022
ARGENTINA 3, FRANCE 3
- Perhaps the greatest football match of all time? Messi completed the set in Doha, Qatar, in one of the all-time great games, as the Albiceleste beat holders France to win a third World Cup. Messi netted twice and once in the shootout, in an epic fitting finale for the little genius.

ANNOUNCING YOURSELF IN STYLE
10 March 2007
BARCELONA 3, REAL MADRID 3
- "It's the Flea with the fast feet and fabulous control who gets closest to el Diego," the *Guardian* declared in the aftermath of yet another young pretender compared to the great Maradona putting on a virtuoso display, as Messi became the first player to score an El Clásico hat-trick in 12 years.

500 AND UP
23 April 2017
REAL MADRID 2, BARCELONA 3
- Messi's records were never-ending and so were the memories. In April 2017's meeting with Real Madrid, Messi struck his fifth century of strikes in what was arguably the most captivating Clásico of all time, with his late winner. The Bernabeu were stunned, as 499 others had been previously.

GOAL OF THIS CENTURY
18 APRIL 2007
BARCELONA 5, GETAFE 2
- The comparisons to Maradona continued when Messi picked up the ball on the same spot of a different pitch to the one that Diego so famously tore England apart from. Comparable to his countryman's Goal of the Century, Messi's Getafe goal has become one of the most iconic post-2000.

RECORD-BREAKER

20 March 2012
BARCELONA 5, GRANADA 3

- Messi was barely hitting his peak by the time he'd broken Barcelona's 60-year scoring record, in yet another La Liga rout in 2012. "I feel sorry for those who want to compete for Messi's throne," manager Pep Guardiola said afterwards. "It's impossible, this kid is unique."

91 IN A YEAR

22 December 2012
VALLADOLID 1, BARCELONA 3

- A record that may never be beaten, Messi netted 91 goals for club and country in a single calendar year, in 12 of the most incredible months of form that anyone had ever seen in the sport. FIFA did not acknowledge the achievement – but the *Guinness World Records* book did.

THE LORD OF LAUDERDALE

21 July 2023
INTER MIAMI 2, CRUZ AZUL 1

- Even after all this time, there is no one quite as box office – even off the bench. Messi's first foray in US soccer was a simple cameo to announce himself to a brave new world and he still stole the show, netting the winner on his Inter Miami debut with a trademark free kick.

HEADING FOR GLORY

27 May 2009
BARCELONA 2, MANCHESTER UNITED 0

- Historians may look back at the difference between Messi and Ronaldo physically and note that the Portuguese was a much better header of a ball – yet to win the Champions League final in 2009, Messi rose above everyone to score with his head... including CR7 on the opposite side.

THE COPA KING

10 July 2021 ARGENTINA 1, BRAZIL 0

- After disappointments and heartbreaks, retirements and frustrations, Messi finally brought silverware back to his home country in the sweetest way possible. Argentina's 2021 Copa América was won at the hands of bitter neighbours Brazil in their backyard, with Messi partying all night in the Maracanã.

THE REIGN IN SPAIN

22 November 2014
BARCELONA 5, SEVILLA 1

- In 2014, Messi dominated Spanish football to become the league's record scorer. He holds the record for most goals scored in a single season in Europe's top five leagues with 50 in 2011-12, and is also the only player to win the league's top scorer award in eight seasons.

THE MIAMI

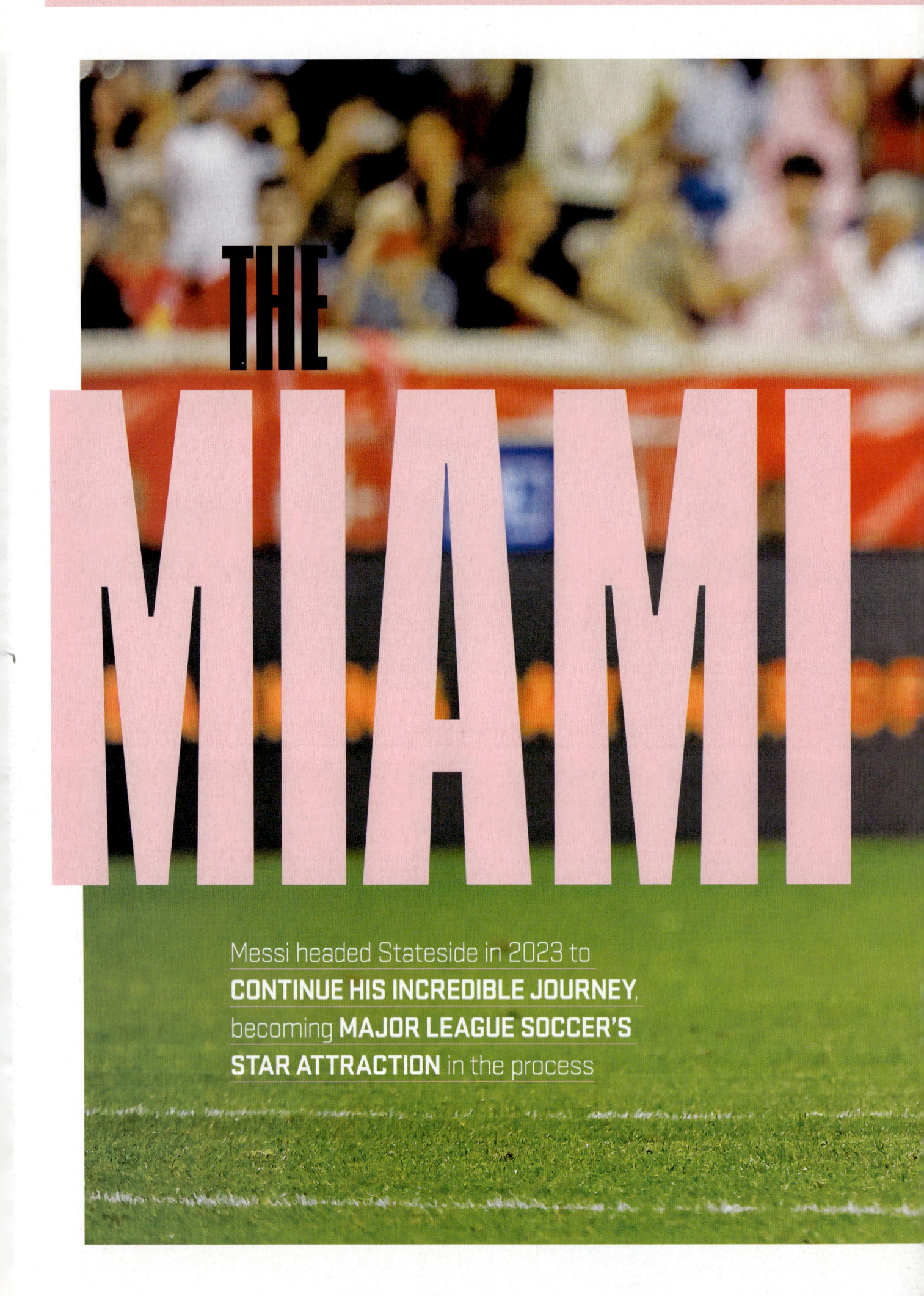

Messi headed Stateside in 2023 to **CONTINUE HIS INCREDIBLE JOURNEY,** becoming **MAJOR LEAGUE SOCCER'S STAR ATTRACTION** in the process

MVP

THE MIAMI MVP

▶ **CO-OWNERS OF INTER** Miami, Jorge Mas, José Mas and David Beckham all stand alongside Lionel Messi after unveiling him as an Inter Miami player in July 2023, following speculation that he could either return to Barcelona or move to Saudi Arabia. However, Messi opted for the MLS and, in a groundbreaking move, was set to earn additional shares from jersey sales, MLS Season Pass subscriptions, and a stake in the club itself.

IMAGE: JOE RAEDLE / GETTY IMAGES

▶ **GETTING THE BAND** back together? Just a day after bringing Barcelona's greatest icon to Florida, Inter Miami added a second in quick succession, signing one of the most celebrated defensive midfielders in a generation, in Sergio Busquets. Not long after that, another ex-Barca star, Jordi Alba, would link up with his former teammates as the Messi era began to really take shape. In December, they would also be joined by another ex-teammate, Luis Suarez.

IMAGE: GIORGIO VIERA / AFP VIA GETTY IMAGES

THE MIAMI MVP

FANS WERE IN CELEBRATORY MOOD AND THE MAN HIMSELF COULDN'T WAIT TO GET STARTED EITHER

MESSI MANIA WAS sweeping across Florida. Fans were in celebratory mood and the man himself couldn't wait to get started either. "I'm very excited to start this next step in my career with Inter Miami and in the United States," Messi said. "This is a fantastic opportunity and together we will continue to build this beautiful project. The idea is to work together to achieve the objectives we set, and I'm very eager to start helping here in my new home."

IMAGE: GIORGIO VIERA / AFP VIA GETTY IMAGES

THE MIAMI MVP

▶

MESSI'S DEBUT WAS set to take place against Cruz Azul in the Leagues Cup, giving the Argentine his bow against Mexican opposition as the city of Miami prepared to welcome the greatest footballer of all time. For a nation that hasn't traditionally been a football powerhouse, to say the least, the excitement across the United States was palpable, to see Messi in action for his new club.

IMAGE: MATTHEW ASHTON - AMA / GETTY IMAGES

◀

MESSI CAME OFF the bench against Cruz Azul – and with the game in the balance at 1-1, he had exactly the kind of impact that he'd had his entire career. Messi buried a free kick to win the match in injury time, as Fort Lauderdale erupted. The GOAT had arrived, all right, with Inter Miami president David Beckham moved to tears following the first-day heroics of his new MVP.

IMAGE: MIKE EHRMANN / GETTY IMAGES

THE MIAMI MVP

MESSI HAD STARTED how he meant to go on in the American soccer scene, netting a brace within 22 minutes of his second game against Atlanta United before Robert Taylor doubled the score with two of his own later on. Inter Miami topped their Leagues Cup group, thanks in part to their new superstar's arrival, smashing their MLS rivals 4-0 and looking reinvigorated with Messi in tow.

IMAGE: GIORGIO VIERA / AFP VIA GETTY IMAGES

INTER MIAMI SPENT four years of planning to bring Lionel Messi to Florida, before two years of pursuing him, stretching back to when he first left Barcelona. The club's co-owner David Beckham stated that the drawn-out recruitment process had been "worth it" prior to Messi's debut – and as pink fireworks lit up the night sky over a sold-out DRV PNK Stadium, it was hard to argue that bringing Messi to Major League Soccer hadn't already proved a success.

IMAGE: MIKE EHRMANN / GETTY IMAGES

THE MIAMI MVP

ANOTHER LEAGUES CUP fixture, another goal scored from a free kick, another thriller. Inter Miami continued to romp through the competition with Messi grabbing himself another two goals, before scoring in a penalty shootout following a 4-4 barnstormer against FC Dallas in Texas. The man for the big occasion was coming up trumps again for his new employers.

IMAGE: JUAN FINOL / GETTY IMAGES

THERE WAS SIMPLY no stopping the GOAT, as he tore up the Leagues Cup with his new side. Another goal against Charlotte FC in the quarter-finals before yet another in the semi-finals against Philadelphia Union punctuated 4-0 and 4-1 victories respectively. But the sheer class and control with which Messi was dominating games was obvious: this was a superstar that the US hadn't seen in a while.

IMAGE: HECTOR VIVAS / GETTY IMAGES

THE MIAMI MVP

IN THE LEAGUES Cup final, Messi once again struck the opening goal and led his side to glory – but it wasn't exactly easy. Away in Nashville, Inter Miami had to toil to victory, with their mercurial No.10 in a free role, barely running across the pitch but still dictating the play with ease. Inter Miami would eventually win on penalties after 11 players on either side took a spot kick.

IMAGE: NICK TRE. SMITH / ICON SPORTSWIRE VIA GETTY IMAGES

THE LEAGUES CUP was Inter Miami's first-ever trophy and the latest in a long line of accolades for their new hero. Out of nowhere, the unfancied Inter Miami had overcome every team in the MLS and Mexico's Liga MX, with Messi taking the Best Player award and netting ten goals over the course of the competition. Talk about making an instant impact.

IMAGE: TIM NWACHUKWU / GETTY IMAGES

THE MIAMI MVP

MESSI'S OPENING SEASON in Major League Soccer ended with a loss away to Charlotte FC – but it had been a huge success, despite Inter Miami's midtable finish. With 11 goals in 14 matches, Messi had delivered an undeniable impact to his new side and shown exactly what he was capable of, despite his age.

IMAGE: MATT KELLEY / GETTY IMAGES

ANOTHER DEBUT, ANOTHER moment of Messi magic. Once again, the Argentine was on hand to lend Inter Miami his genius, coming on as a substitute for his Major League Soccer debut against New York Red Bulls and scoring in a 2-0 win. The goal was a picturesque moment of brilliance from the GOAT, ending Inter Miami's run of 11 league matches without a win.

IMAGE: AL BELLO / GETTY IMAGES

THE GOAL WAS A MOMENT OF BRILLIANCE FROM THE GOAT

THE MIAMI MVP

DID YOU KNOW

Leo Messi must speak Spanish to Inter Miami co-owner David Beckham, since the Argentine is said to understand English but not confidently speak very much of the language. Beckham – who played for PSG, just as Messi did – can speak a little Spanish, thanks to his time at Real Madrid. The two icons met on the pitch as players, though for Beckham to favour Messi over Ronaldo, considering he played for two of CR7's clubs, is a little ironic. In a community survey in 2017, 70 per cent of Miami said they spoke Spanish at home – meaning Messi can probably get by in the city.

IMAGE: MEGAN BRIGGS / GETTY IMAGES

EVEN THOUGH HIS style of play had changed considerably in his mid-30s, Messi had proven that he was capable of dazzling brilliance in the United States, being the undisputed superstar of Major League Soccer. With crowds flocking to see the GOAT in action and American audiences captivated by a legend, Beckham and co had shown there was an appetite for Messi in the country.

IMAGE: RICH STORRY / GETTY IMAGES

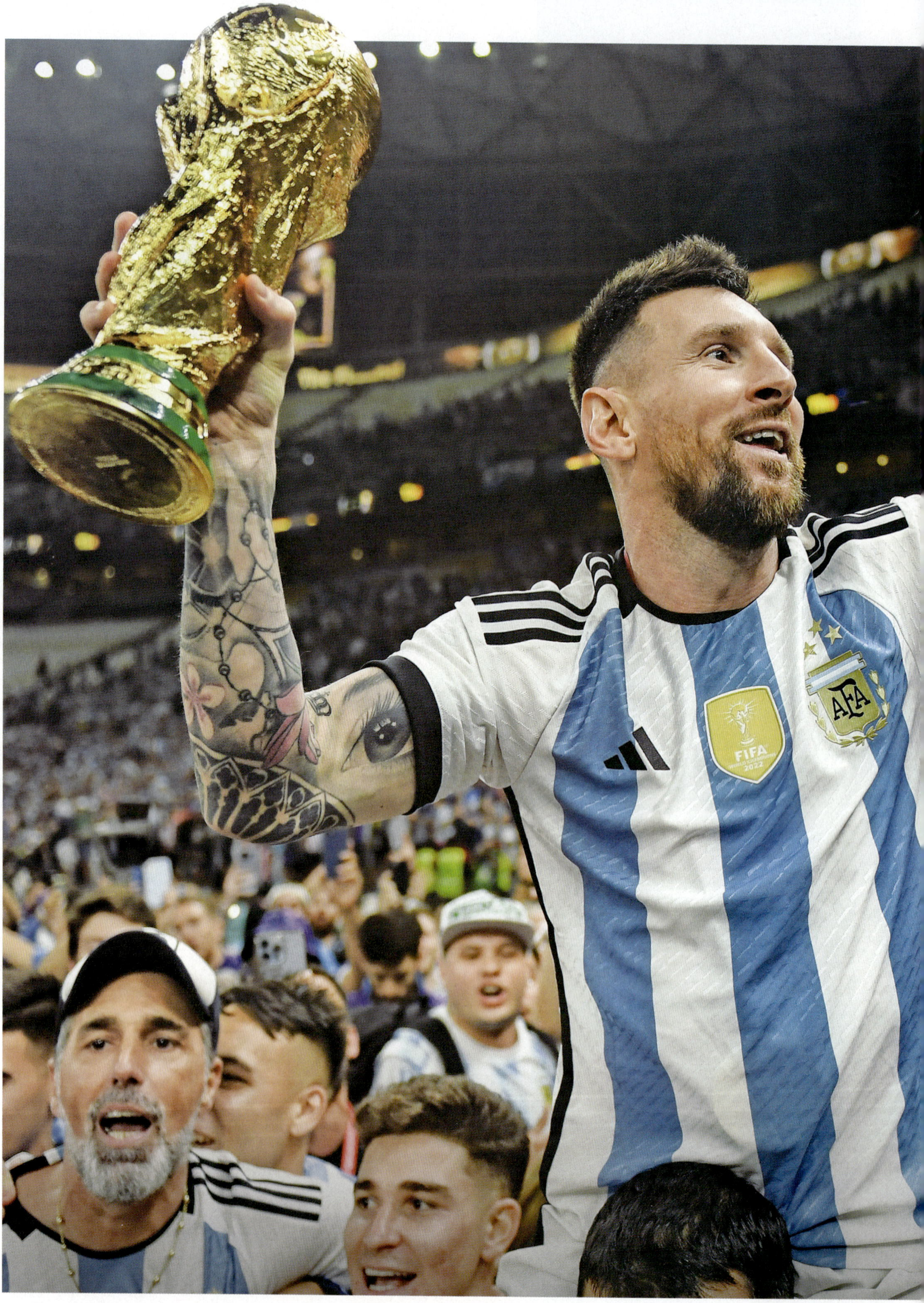
FIFA
AFA

After years of frustration, some wondered if the **WORLD'S GREATEST PLAYER** would ever get his hands on **FOOTBALL'S BIGGEST PRIZE...**

ARGENTINA'S NEW MESSIAH

ARGENTINA'S NEW MESSIAH

▼ COMPARISONS TO DIEGO Maradona aren't exactly dished out often. In 2005, a young Lionel Messi won the under-20 World Cup with Argentina with a No.18 on his back, picking up the Golden Boot and the Golden Ball. The hype for this youngster was through the stratosphere. Maradona himself had won the tournament decades before. Naturally, it was Messi who netted two penalties in the final to lift the trophy.

IMAGE: ARIS MESSINIS / AFP VIA GETTY IMAGES

▲ WHILE EXCITEMENT TO see Messi make his international debut was high, it didn't exactly last long. The wonderkid was dismissed against Hungary during his first senior start for his country after touching the ball once and flinging out an elbow in reaction to a tackle from a Hungarian defender. Messi would only be sent off another two times in his career.

IMAGE: MICHAEL MAYHEW / ALLSTAR / GETTY IMAGES

THE BBC'S ALAN Hansen picked the entire Argentina side for his Team of the Tournament at the midway point of the 2006 World Cup: the Albiceleste were so graceful and deadly that they tore the group stage apart and scored one of the greatest team goals ever seen at a World Cup against Serbia and Montenegro. But then came the heartbreak, with hosts Germany knocking them out in the quarter-finals before tempers flared at full-time. Coach José Pékerman was roundly criticised for not bringing on Messi in the defeat.

IMAGE: JUNG YEON-JE / AFP VIA GETTY IMAGES

ARGENTINA WERE MUCH stronger than rivals Brazil in 2007: if fans wondered how they hadn't won the World Cup in 2006, they were still scratching their heads at the Copa América a year later. A depleted Seleção scooped the trophy after beating Argentina 3-0 in the final with Messi's Brazilian wonderkid equivalent, Robinho, the tournament's top scorer and best player. This was about the last time that the pair would be even close to comparable, however, with their careers about to take rather radically different trajectories...

IMAGE: LUIS ACOSTA / AFP VIA GETTY IMAGES

BARCELONA DIDN'T WANT Messi to go to Beijing to compete in the 2008 Olympics, in what was essentially a youth tournament. Manager Pep Guardiola gave his blessing, however, and it resulted in Messi – alongside Sergio Agüero (pictured with Messi), Juan Riquelme and Ángel Di María – bringing the gold back for the South Americans. It was a golden generation in waiting, with hopes high that these youngsters could deliver on the senior stage one day.

IMAGE: KOJI WATANABE / GETTY IMAGES

ARGENTINA'S NEW MESSIAH

UNDER THE MANAGEMENT of maverick Diego Maradona, Messi's Argentina endured another tough World Cup in 2010 – making it out of the group, at least, but getting hammered 4-0 and going out at the hands of the Germans once more in the quarter-finals. It wasn't a vintage Argentine side by any stretch, however – and 2010 remains the only World Cup that Messi went to but didn't score at.

IMAGE: RICHARD HEATHCOTE / GETTY IMAGES

IN 2011, IT became official: the hopes of the nation were on Messi's shoulders, with the skipper's armband his, too. In being given the honour of leading his country, he became a different kind of captain to Javier Mascherano, assuming a quieter leadership style – but in time, he would be capable of speaking up and leading his country through words as well as actions.

IMAGE: VALENTINO ROSSI / LATINCONTENT VIA GETTY IMAGES

ONCE AGAIN, IT was Germany who broke Messi's heart, this time at the 2014 World Cup in Brazil. Argentina had no right to be competing on the same level as a generational Die Mannschaft side who had dismantled Brazil 7-1 in their semi-final. Messi, meanwhile, dragged his nation to the final at the Maracanã only for them to lose 1-0 after extra time. Some suggested he'd been subdued at the tournament but his creative influence had been huge, and he was awarded the tournament's Golden Ball.

IMAGE: SIMON BRUTY / ANYCHANCE / GETTY IMAGES

BY NOW, MESSI was beginning to think he was cursed. In 2015, the Copa América rolled around and Argentina once again made the final, only for an Alexis Sánchez-inspired Chile to sweep to victory. It looked as though the greatest footballer of a generation would finish his career without any silverware to show for his international exploits, with some by now suggesting he'd have been better off playing for Spain.

IMAGE: MIGUEL TOVAR / LATINCONTENT VIA GETTY IMAGES

THE FINAL STRAW. In the 100-year anniversary of the Copa América in 2016, Chile and Argentina again reached the showpiece in what looked like fate arranging the rematch in order to give the Albiceleste their opportunity to exact revenge. Once again, however, Argentina lost out in a heartbreaking shootout. It was too much to take for Argentina's crestfallen captain, who announced his international retirement in the wake of the result.

IMAGE: HECTOR VIVAS / LATINCONTENT VIA GETTY IMAGES

MESSI HAD UNFINISHED business with Argentina, however. As much as the international failure had broken his heart time and again – three finals in as many years – he wasn't exactly a quitter. Come qualification for the 2018 World Cup, the captain was back in the fold and looking to make amends. A national campaign to get him to change his mind may have helped: only Leo knows.

IMAGE: JUAN MABROMATA / GETTY IMAGES

ARGENTINA WERE NOWHERE NEAR THE QUALITY OF THE EUROPEAN NATIONS

ARGUABLY THE LIMPEST World Cup exit of them all. In 2018, Argentina struggled through the group stage, despite Messi scoring a wonderful goal against Nigeria, only to be battered by eventual winners France and a young Kylian Mbappé. Messi was starting to look old and tired. Argentina were nowhere near the quality of the European nations, with the upcoming 2022 World Cup marking two decades since a South American world champion.

IMAGE: ALEXANDER HASSENSTEIN / GETTY IMAGES

ARGENTINA'S NEW MESSIAH

AT WEMBLEY IN the summer of 2022, the South American champions, Argentina, took on the European champions, Italy. The Albiceleste were rampant, running out 3-0 winners and looking like the best team on Earth, with Messi looking freer than ever from the shackles of expectation that have always come from playing for his nation. It's a nice way to warm up for a World Cup, isn't it?

IMAGE: UEFA / UEFA VIA GETTY IMAGES

FINALLY, GLORY ON the international stage for Messi, at the 2021 Copa América. Once again, the Albiceleste were taken to a penalty shootout along the way, only to present an ace card this time around in goalkeeper Emi Martínez. Just as at the Beijing Olympics, it was Ángel Di María who struck the winner in the final, while Messi capped off the first time he'd won an international tournament as the joint top scorer and with the Best Player award to boot.

IMAGE: CARL DE SOUZA / GETTY IMAGES

ARGENTINA'S NEW MESSIAH

🔽 **A RESULT SO** momentous, that a national holiday in Saudi Arabia was declared off the back of it. In Argentina's first 2022 World Cup game, Messi and co slumped to a historic defeat at the hands of the Middle Eastern nation, despite VAR intervening to stop it from becoming a cricket score in the South Americans' favour. That was supposed to be the easiest game of the group...

IMAGE: MATTHIAS HANGST / GETTY IMAGES

▶ **IF ANYONE CAN** rise to the occasion, it's Messi. In the crunch fixture against Mexico, he rose higher than anyone else to drag Argentina back into contention with a superb finish. It was almost as if he was refusing to let history repeat itself, instead looking to take matters into his own hands. After beating Mexico, a 2-0 win over Poland meant Argentina would qualify from their group as winners, in the end.

IMAGE: DAN MULLAN / GETTY IMAGES

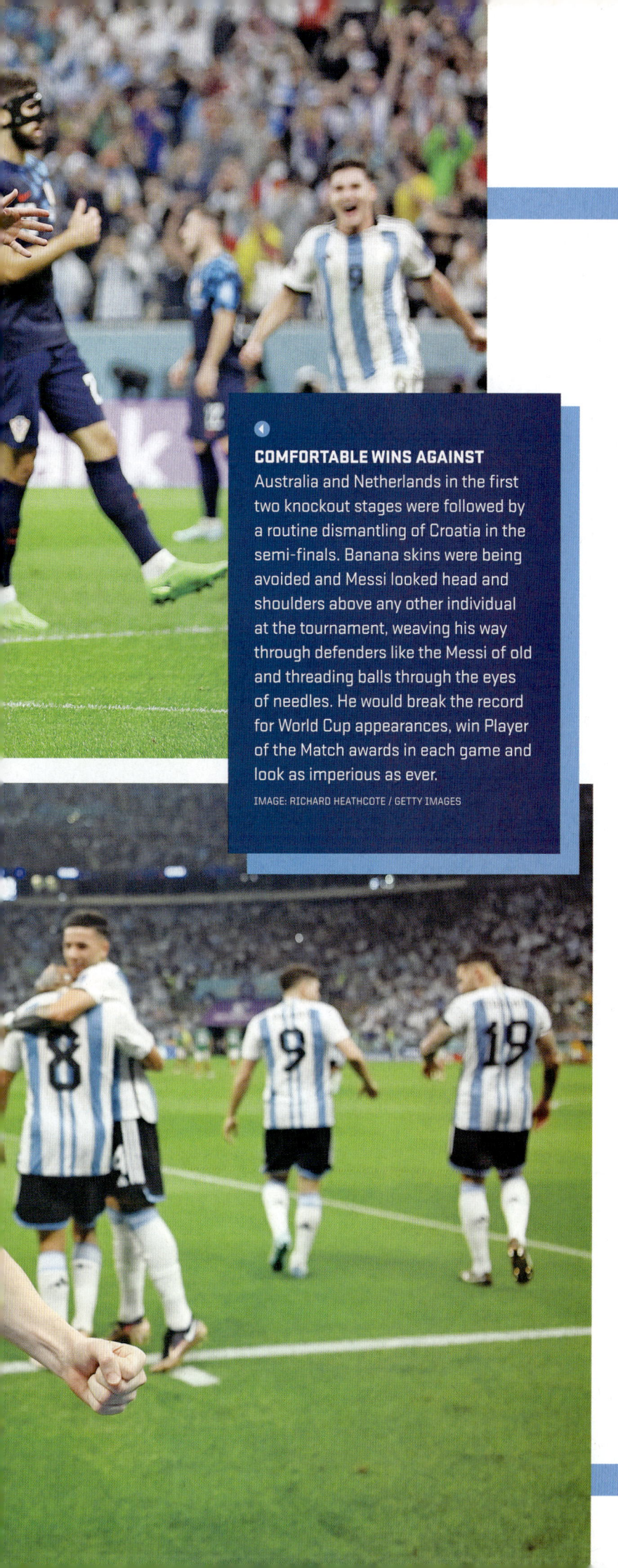

COMFORTABLE WINS AGAINST
Australia and Netherlands in the first two knockout stages were followed by a routine dismantling of Croatia in the semi-finals. Banana skins were being avoided and Messi looked head and shoulders above any other individual at the tournament, weaving his way through defenders like the Messi of old and threading balls through the eyes of needles. He would break the record for World Cup appearances, win Player of the Match awards in each game and look as imperious as ever.

IMAGE: RICHARD HEATHCOTE / GETTY IMAGES

DID YOU KNOW

For an international career once deemed a disappointment, he's come a long way. Messi has more minutes at the World Cup than anyone else; is the only player to score in all five rounds of the tournament; has the most assists at a World Cup; most goals at major international tournaments; while he's won the big three – a Copa, World Cup and Olympics – oh, and he's Argentina's record appearance holder and scorer. "Did it annoy me that Messi took the [scoring] record?" Gabriel Batistuta once pondered. "A little, yes. But the advantage I have is that I'm second to an extraterrestrial."

IMAGE: MARCELO ENDELLI/GETTY IMAGES

ARGENTINA'S NEW MESSIAH

ARGENTINA WOULD FACE France in arguably the greatest final ever. Messi gave Argentina the lead, Di María extended it and Mbappé struck twice to level things, as the old master and the new pretender went head to head. Messi thought he'd won it in extra time, but Mbappé equalised once again – before Argentina won on penalties. Messi became the first man ever to win two Golden Balls at World Cups. This was his tournament.

IMAGE: CLIVE BRUNSKILL / GETTY IMAGES

FINALLY, MESSI WAS on top of the world: undisputed, now, as the greatest who ever lived. After five World Cups, he had lifted the trophy he'd craved more than any other and few could deny that he'd done so as the best player at the tournament – it was arguably the best individual World Cup in history. He had mesmerised, finally getting his hands on the ultimate prize.

IMAGE: DAN MULLAN / GETTY IMAGES

ARGENTINA'S NEW MESSIAH

IT WAS ARGUABLY THE BEST INDIVIDUAL WORLD CUP IN HISTORY

EVEN POST-WORLD Cup, there's no stopping him. He led Argentina to an unprecedented victory against rivals Brazil in the Maracanã a year after the 2022 World Cup – and who can say whether he'll be at the next tournament? Nothing is past the GOAT, after all: he fought all the odds at international level and found himself crowned the best.

IMAGE: WAGNER MEIER / GETTY IMAGES

MESSI BY NUMBERS

Messi's career is not over yet, but here are some of the **KEY NUMBERS** he has compiled so far...

HEIGHT
5'7" (170cm)

WEIGHT
159 lbs (72 kg)

LEFT FOOTED

SHIRT NUMBER
NUMBER 10

MAIN POSITION
- RW — RIGHT WINGER

OTHER POSITIONS
- CF — CENTRE FORWARD
- SS — SECOND STRIKER

SENIOR CLUB DEBUT
16 OCTOBER 2004
AGE 17 YEARS 114 DAYS
BARCELONA VS ESPANYOL

SENIOR INTERNATIONAL DEBUT
17 AUGUST 2005
AGE 18 YEARS 55 DAYS
ARGENTINA VS HUNGARY

MAJOR HONOURS

ARGENTINA

1 WORLD CUP
1 COPA AMÉRICA
1 OLYMPIC GOLD

BARCELONA

4 CHAMPIONS LEAGUE
10 LA LIGA
7 COPA DEL REY

PSG

2 LIGUE 1

INTER MIAMI

1 LEAGUES CUP

KEY RECORDS

8 MOST BALLON D'OR AWARDS

6 MOST EUROPEAN GOLDEN BOOT AWARDS

91 MOST GOALS IN A CALENDAR YEAR 2012

44 MOST OFFICIAL TOP LEVEL TEAM TROPHIES WON

21 MOST CONSECUTIVE LEAGUE MATCHES SCORED IN (RESULTING IN 33 GOALS – 2012-13)

MOST OFFICIAL SENIOR GOALS FOR A SINGLE CLUB (BARCELONA) 672

MOST GOALS IN A SINGLE TOP FLIGHT LEAGUE (LA LIGA) 474

26 MOST WORLD CUP APPEARANCES

21 MOST WORLD CUP GOAL CONTRIBUTIONS (13 GOALS, 8 ASSISTS)

2,314 MOST WORLD CUP MINUTES

TOTAL CAREER STATS

APPEARANCES **1,047**
GOALS **821**
ASSISTS **361**
HAT-TRICKS **57**

0.78 GOALS PER GAME
104.8 MINS PER GOAL
72.8 MINS PER GOAL CONTRIBUTION

3 RED CARDS
96 YELLOW CARDS
INT. CAPS **180**
INT. GOALS **106**

Market Value

CURRENT VALUE **€35 MILLION**
HIGHEST VALUE **€180 MILLION** (1 JANUARY 2018)

GOALS

INSIDE THE BOX **556**
PENALTIES **108**
OUTSIDE THE BOX **92**
FREE KICKS **65**

LEFT FOOT **687**
RIGHT FOOT **105**
HEADERS **26**
OTHER **3**

*All figures correct as of the end of 2023. Figures compiled using data from www.messivsronaldo.app, www.messi.com and www.transfermarkt.co.uk

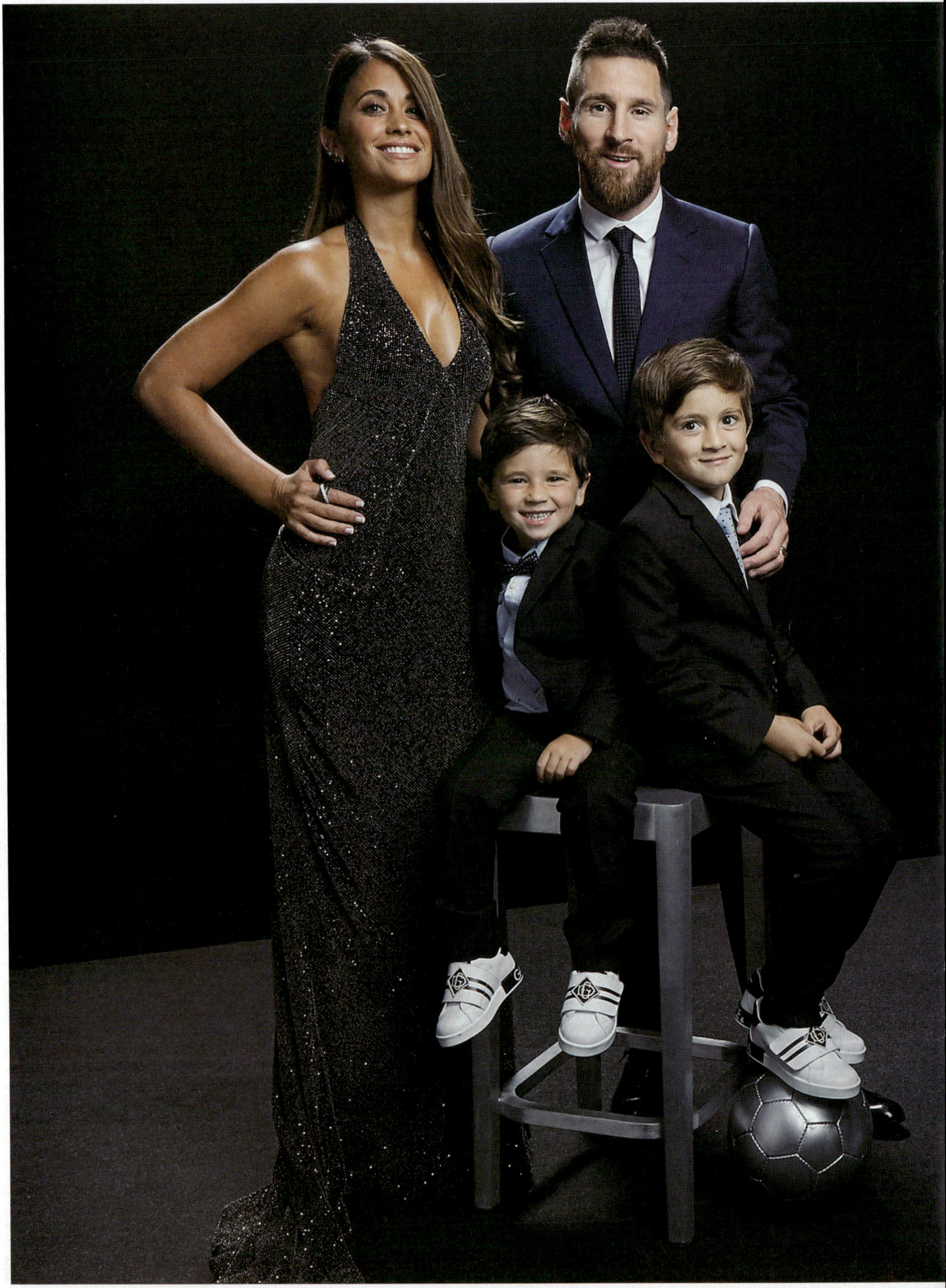

OFF THE PITCH

The man who **COMPLETED EVERYTHING ON THE PITCH** is an interesting and introverted **CHARACTER OFF IT...**

OFF THE PITCH

SINCE THE MID-2000s, Messi has been signed to German brand Adidas, opposite Nike superstar, Cristiano Ronaldo. The Argentine has worn the manufacturer's F50 and X boots as the major face of the brand, with special edition boots given to him exclusively. At the 2022 World Cup, for example, Messi's first world title was capped while donning gold versions of Adidas's X boots of that year.

IMAGE: DAVID RAMOS / GETTY IMAGES FOR ADIDAS

OVER THE YEARS, Messi has featured on EA Sports' iconic *FIFA* series of video games, as well as its major rival, *Pro Evolution Soccer*. The Argentine's appearance as the cover star coincided with his brilliant best at Barcelona, as he became the face of four games, from *FIFA 13* to *FIFA 16*. Messi's former teammate Ronaldinho managed one more cover, with five, while England hero Wayne Rooney has the record with seven.

IMAGE: VISIONHAUS / CORBIS VIA GETTY IMAGES

OFF THE PITCH

MESSI IS ONE of Pepsi's biggest brand ambassadors, continuing the soft drink's tradition of including some of the brightest and best footballers on Earth in its marketing campaigns. The likes of David Beckham and Roberto Carlos have featured in Pepsi commercials, while Messi has been featured starring alongside players such as Vinicius Jr and Paul Pogba, as an undisputed A-lister in the company's promo campaigns.

IMAGE: CLIVE BRUNSKILL / PEPSI VIA GETTY IMAGES

MESSI IS A GLOBAL BRAND IN HIS OWN RIGHT, LENDING HIS NAME AND FACE TO A HOST OF COMPANIES

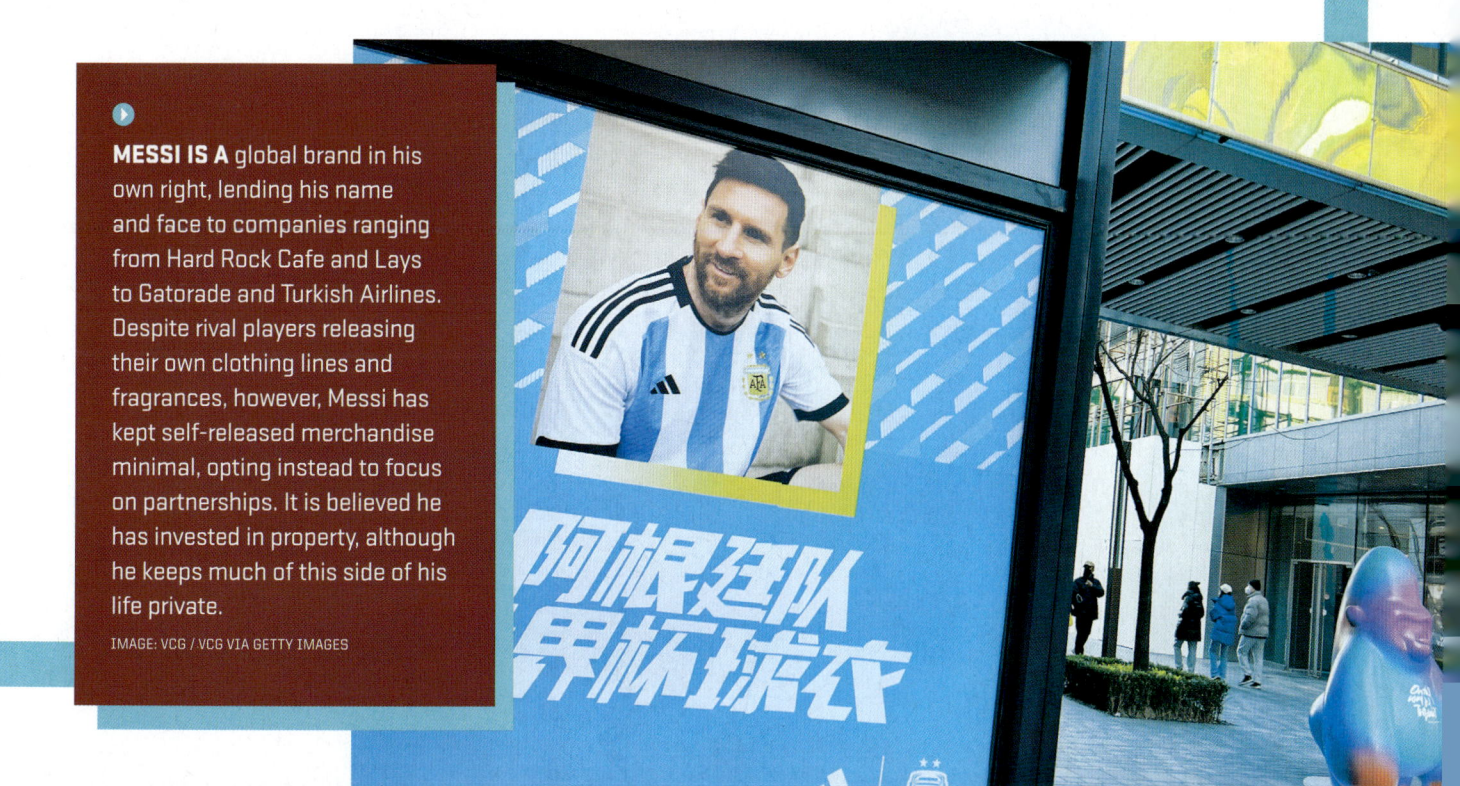

MESSI IS A global brand in his own right, lending his name and face to companies ranging from Hard Rock Cafe and Lays to Gatorade and Turkish Airlines. Despite rival players releasing their own clothing lines and fragrances, however, Messi has kept self-released merchandise minimal, opting instead to focus on partnerships. It is believed he has invested in property, although he keeps much of this side of his life private.

IMAGE: VCG / VCG VIA GETTY IMAGES

DID YOU KNOW

Messi and Cristiano Ronaldo have spent their entire careers as rivals, compared continuously as players – and there's an incredible coincidence between the two GOATs of this generation. Messi was born on 24 June 1987, a whole 869 days after Ronaldo, who was born on 5 February 1985. Leo and his wife Antonela, meanwhile, welcomed their first child, Thiago, into the world on 2 November 2012... exactly 869 days after Cristiano Ronaldo Jr was born on 17 June 2010. Could it be the football world is destined to repeat itself, with two more icons of the next generation going head-to-head with one another?

IMAGE: NICOLÒ CAMPO / LIGHTROCKET VIA GETTY IMAGES

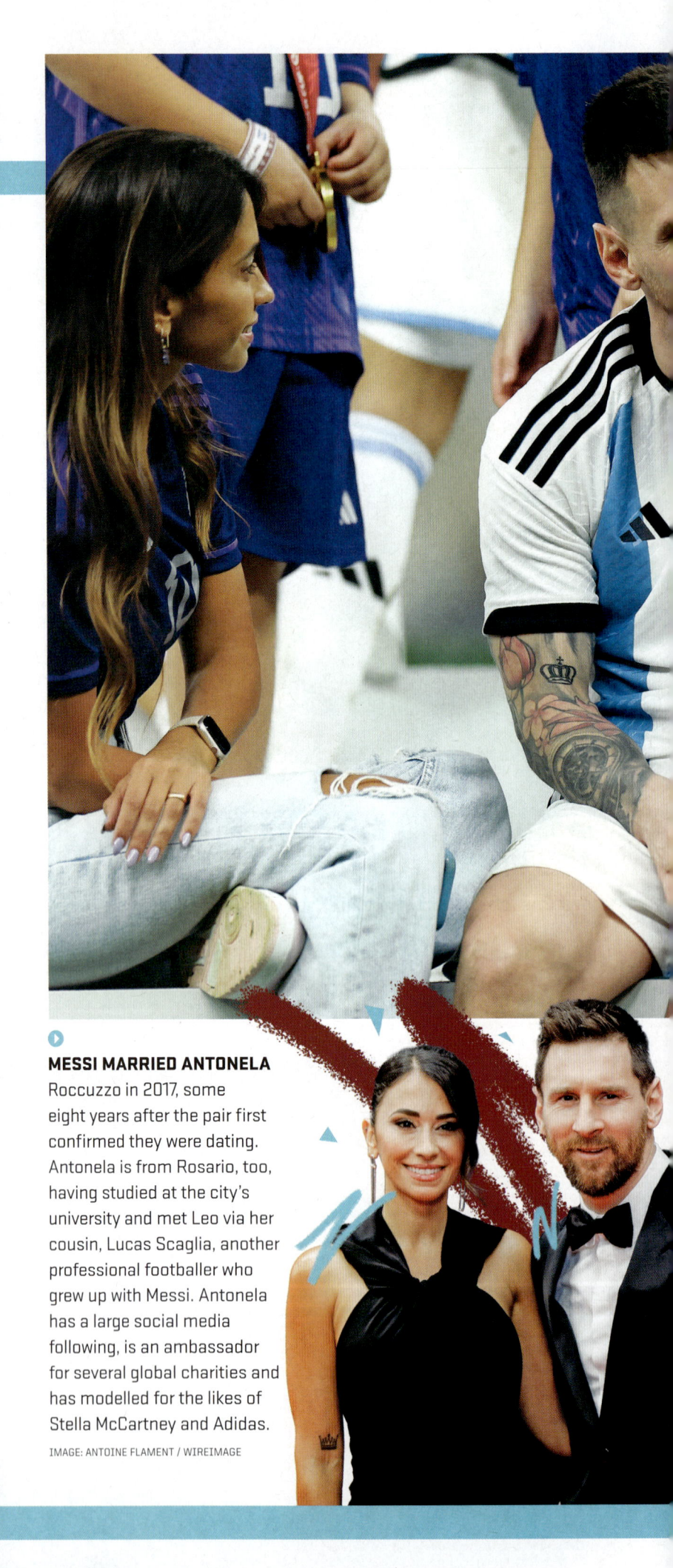

MESSI MARRIED ANTONELA Roccuzzo in 2017, some eight years after the pair first confirmed they were dating. Antonela is from Rosario, too, having studied at the city's university and met Leo via her cousin, Lucas Scaglia, another professional footballer who grew up with Messi. Antonela has a large social media following, is an ambassador for several global charities and has modelled for the likes of Stella McCartney and Adidas.

IMAGE: ANTOINE FLAMENT / WIREIMAGE

OFF THE PITCH

▸ **MESSI AND HIS** wife Antonela have three children together. The pair welcomed their first son, Thiago, in 2012, with their second son, Mateo, being born three years later in 2015. Their third son, Ciro, arrived in 2018, another three years later. Messi has spoken in the past about how fatherhood has changed him as a person, saying in 2019, "as a human being, having three children changed my way of thinking and it also helped me grow".

IMAGE: MAJA HITIJ - FIFA / FIFA VIA GETTY IMAGES

▸ **LEO'S FATHER JORGE** is one of the most notable agents in football, responsible for handling his son's career in the sport since the age of 14 and being a principle driver in his moves to PSG and Inter Miami. The rest of Messi's life is run as a family business. Eldest brother Rodrigo is responsible for Leo's publicity, while his other brother, Matías, runs the Leo Messi Foundation with his mother, Celia.

IMAGE: JOSEP LAGO / GETTY IMAGES

OFF THE PITCH

SINCE 2004, MESSI has contributed his time and finances to the United Nations Children's Fund (UNICEF), becoming a goodwill ambassador and participating in various campaigns concerning subjects such as HIV prevention, education and disadvantaged and disabled children. The UNICEF organisation has a close relationship with Barcelona as a football club, becoming the first logo to feature across the iconic Blaugrana shirts.

IMAGE: JOSEP LAGO / AFP VIA GETTY IMAGES

THE LEO MESSI Foundation was set up in 2007, following Messi visiting a hospital for terminally ill children in Boston, United States. The Argentine decided that he wanted to donate a portion of his earnings to charity and sought to provide access for children to health care and education, as well as sport. Messi has awarded research grants and invested in medical training and projects in Argentina, via his foundation.

IMAGE: LALO YASKY / GETTY IMAGES

OFF THE PITCH

MESSI IS CLOSE friends with former Manchester City star Sergio 'Kun' Agüero, and roomed with the striker while on international duty since the pair of them were in Argentina's youth sides. Messi is godfather to Agüero's son, Benjamin, too – and though the pair have both played for Barcelona, King Kun joined the Catalan club just weeks before Messi sealed his transfer to PSG.

IMAGE: DAVID RAMOS - FIFA / FIFA VIA GETTY IMAGES

MESSI HAS ALSO given back to youth football in his home country. He financially supports Sarmiento, a football club based in Rosario where his former coach Ernesto Vecchio (pictured above) worked, while he has helped refurbish facilities not just at his boyhood club of Newell's Old Boys, but local rivals Rosario Central, as well as River Plate and Boca Juniors in Buenos Aires.

IMAGE: CARLOS CARRION / AFP VIA GETTY IMAGES

HE DECIDED HE WANTED TO DONATE A PORTION OF HIS EARNINGS TO CHARITY

IN 2021, MESSI helped to obtain 50,000 COVID-19 vaccines from Chinese company Sinovac Biotech in a plan to inoculate all of South America's footballers before the Copa América of that year. Messi was left with after-effects of contracting COVID and wanted to ensure that all players from his home continent were vaccinated, by donating three signed shirts.

IMAGE: NELSON ALMEIDA / AFP VIA GETTY IMAGES

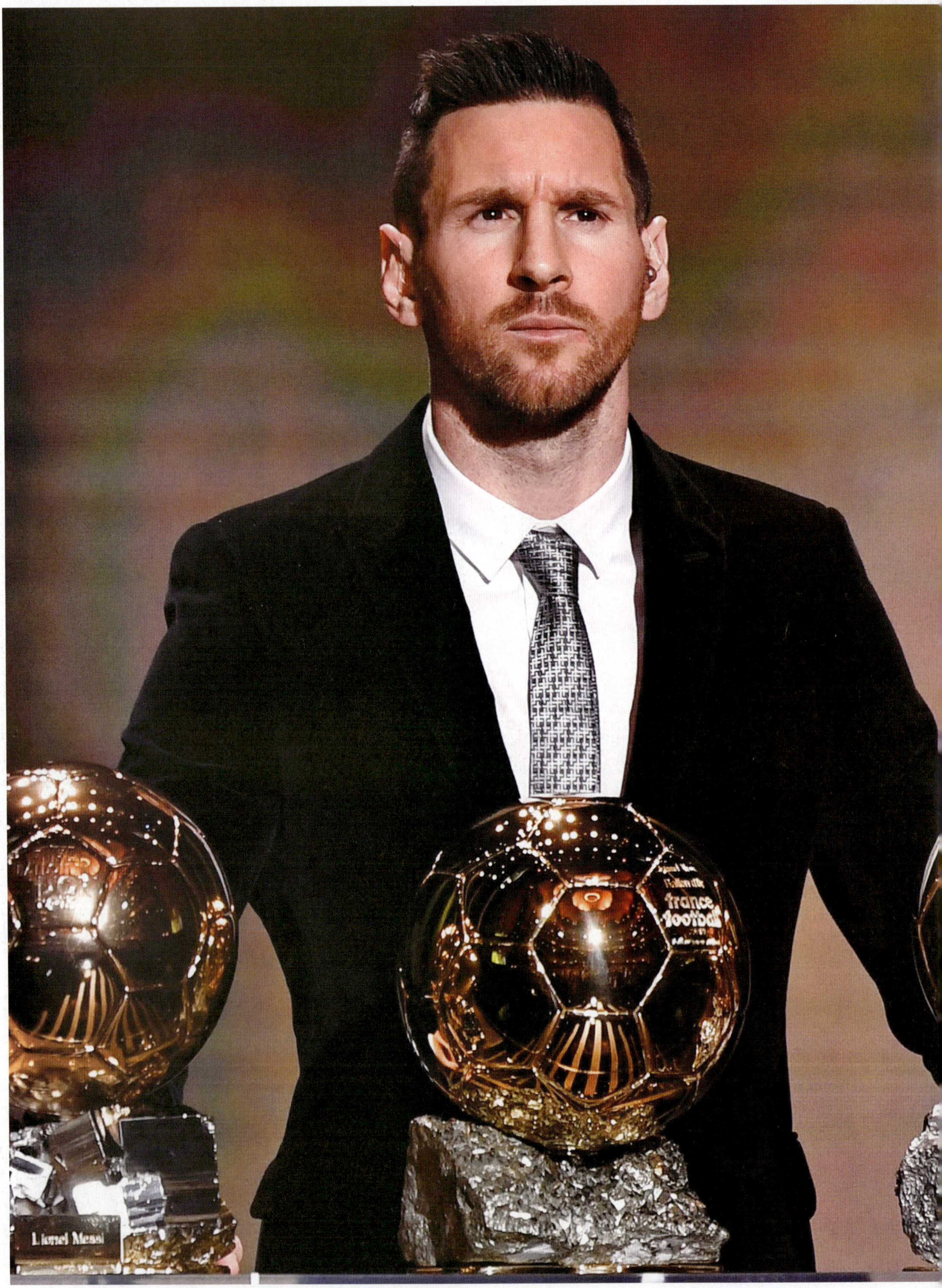
france football
Lionel Messi

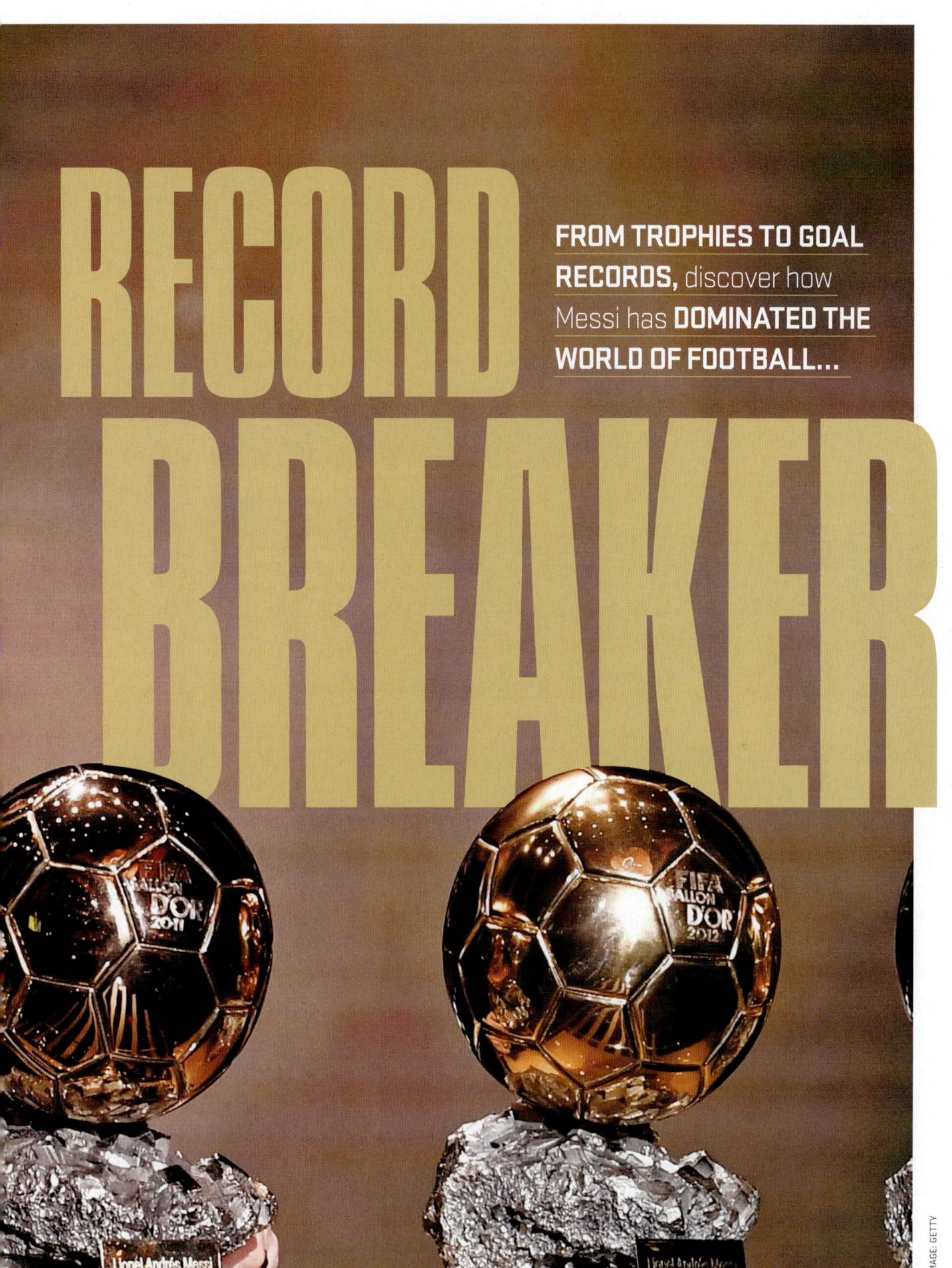

RECORD BREAKER

FROM TROPHIES TO GOAL RECORDS, discover how Messi has **DOMINATED THE WORLD OF FOOTBALL...**

RECORD BREAKER

▶ **AFTER COMING THIRD** in the 2007 Ballon d'Or to Kaká and second in 2008 to long-term rival Cristiano Ronaldo, Messi won his first of the award in 2009, following Barcelona's incredible six-trophy haul of that year. He garnered 473 of the final votes, double what Ronaldo managed for second place, following his move to Real Madrid. Teammate Xavi Hernandez finished third in the award's polling.

IMAGE: DENIS DOYLE / GETTY IMAGES

◀ **DESPITE SPAIN WINNING** the World Cup in 2010 and Inter Milan lifting a Treble under José Mourinho, Messi was crowned Ballon d'Or winner in 2010 for the second year in a row. That year was a special one for Barcelona, as all three players on the podium came through the famed La Masia academy. Messi received 22 per cent of the vote ahead of Andrés Iniesta and Xavi with 17 and 16, respectively.

IMAGE: STUART FRANKLIN - FIFA / FIFA VIA GETTY IMAGES

MESSI GARNERED 473 OF THE FINAL VOTES, DOUBLE WHAT RONALDO MANAGED

RECORD BREAKER

A THIRD CONSECUTIVE Ballon d'Or followed for Messi in 2011, after Barça again lifted the Champions League trophy. Ronaldo once again finished second, Xavi once again third, as Messi became just the fourth player to win three of the awards; he'd lift a fourth in 2012, beating Ronaldo in second and Iniesta in third to the award, to cap a dynasty as Ballon d'Or champion.

IMAGE: STUART FRANKLIN - FIFA / FIFA VIA GETTY IMAGES

THE TREBLE WITH Barcelona in 2015 was capped off nicely with a fifth Ballon d'Or for Messi, after Ronaldo had won two of his own in quick succession. Ronaldo was once again second to Messi, with Barça teammate Neymar in third. This was the last time that the award would be branded with FIFA's name, reverting back to the France Football Ballon d'Or for 2016.

IMAGE: DAVID RAMOS / GETTY IMAGES

A RECORD SIXTH Ballon d'Or was awarded to Messi in 2019. The award took a COVID-enforced hiatus in 2020, before Messi lifted his seventh in 2021, this time with Paris Saint-Germain. While the award had been overwhelmingly awarded to the Argentine in previous years, the competition was a lot tougher this time. Virgil van Dijk finished second in 2019, Robert Lewandowski controversially so in 2021.

IMAGE: FRANCK FIFE / AFP VIA GETTY IMAGES

DID YOU KNOW

When it comes to which nation has the most Ballon d'Or triumphs, Argentina is top of the league – which is impressive, considering the gong was European-only for its first 39 years. Talk about getting a head start. This record is, once again, thanks to Messi. France, Germany, Netherlands and Portugal all have seven wins each – but while five French players, five Germans, three Dutchmen and three Portuguese have won the award... one Argentine has lifted it eight times all on his own. Complete dominance and proof that Messi is as good as at least five others.

IMAGE: AURELIEN MEUNIER / GETTY IMAGES

MESSI'S EIGHTH BALLON d'Or, presented to him by David Beckham in 2023, set him in a class of his own. Awarded after winning a World Cup in 2022, Messi became the first man to have won the award while playing outside Europe – and the first player to have scooped three gongs at three separate clubs. Next-generation talents Erling Haaland and Kylian Mbappé finished second and third respectively.

IMAGE: MEGAN BRIGGS / GETTY IMAGES

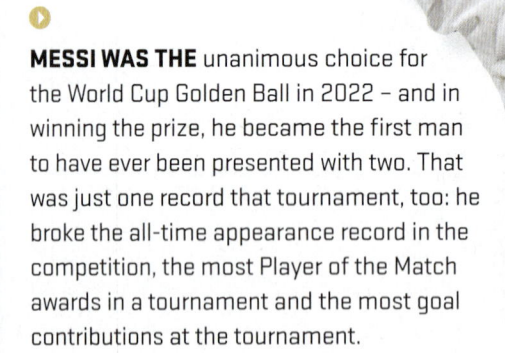

MESSI WAS THE unanimous choice for the World Cup Golden Ball in 2022 – and in winning the prize, he became the first man to have ever been presented with two. That was just one record that tournament, too: he broke the all-time appearance record in the competition, the most Player of the Match awards in a tournament and the most goal contributions at the tournament.

IMAGE: CLIVE BRUNSKILL / GETTY IMAGES

MESSI'S EIGHTH BALLON D'OR IN 2023 SET HIM IN A CLASS OF HIS OWN

WITH EIGHT PICHICHI awards – the trophy handed out to the top scorer of La Liga every season – Messi has more than any other player, as well as having the all-time scoring record in the Spanish top tier, to boot. Messi is also the top assist provider in La Liga with 192, has struck the most goals in a La Liga season with 50 and was the first man to reach 450 La Liga goals.

IMAGE: LLUIS GENE / AFP VIA GETTY IMAGES

- **HAVING NETTED OVER** 820 professional goals for club and country throughout his career, it's perhaps no surprise that Messi is also the first and only player in history to win five and six European Golden Shoes, the award given to the top scorer across Europe. Since a points system was established for league difficulty, Messi holds the record for the most ever in a season, with 100 for his 50 league goal haul of 2011-12.

IMAGE: JAVIER SORIANO / AFP VIA GETTY IMAGES

RECORD BREAKER

MESSI HAS THE most caps and goals for Argentina, among a plethora of other notable achievements. He was the youngest player to play and score for Argentina at a World Cup and the only Argentina player to score against every CONMEBOL nation. He's played in more World Cups than any other Argentine and more Copa Américas, too. He also has the most hat-tricks, assists and goals from free-kicks of anyone from the Albiceleste.

IMAGE: BOB LEVEY / GETTY IMAGES

WITH FOUR CHAMPIONS League titles, Messi has dominated the competition – and has some intriguing stats to match. He has the most goals for one club (that's 120 for Barça), the most number of opponents scored against with 40 and the most goals scored in a game, for his five-star performance against Bayer Leverkusen. He became the youngest player to score 50 in the Champions League when he was 24, too.

IMAGE: STEPHANE DANNA / AFP VIA GETTY IMAGES

HE BECAME THE YOUNGEST PLAYER TO SCORE 50 IN THE CHAMPIONS LEAGUE

RECORD BREAKER

▸ **OTHER RECORDS TUMBLE** at Messi's feet. Despite never winning the Puskás Award for best goal of a calendar year, he has more nominations than anyone, with seven. He has the most Player of the Year awards for *FourFourTwo*, the *Guardian* and *World Soccer* – and he is the only player to win a 'Best Player/Golden Ball' award at all official tournaments he's played at (the U-20 World Cup, World Cup and Copa América).

IMAGE: MIGUEL RUIZ / FC BARCELONA VIA GETTY IMAGES

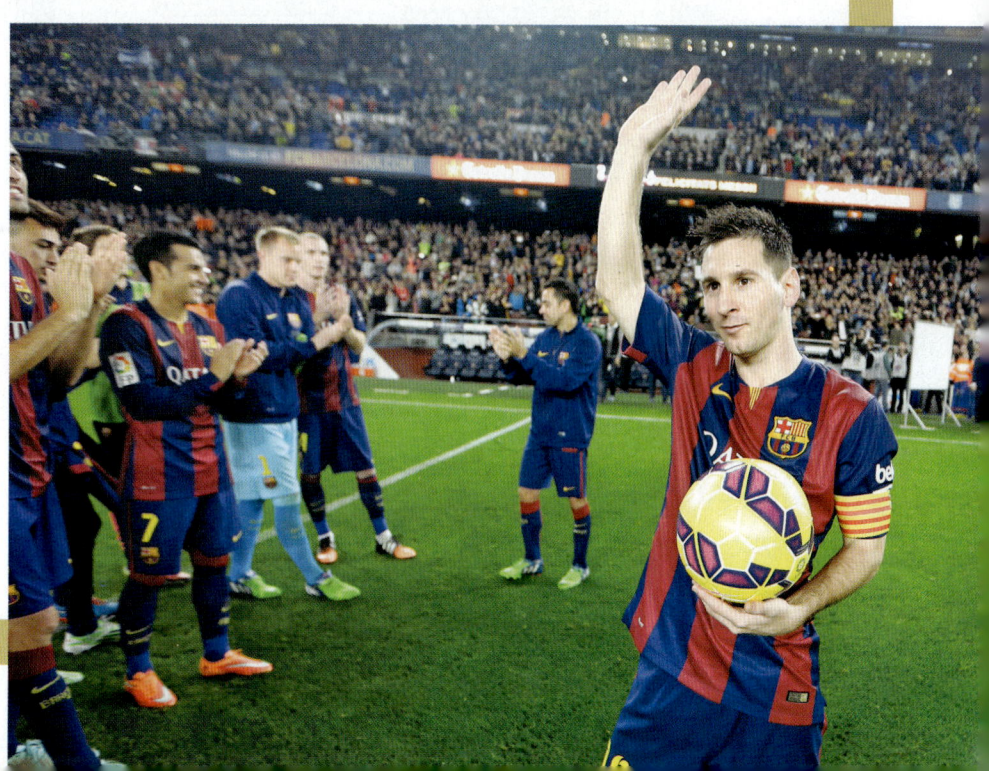

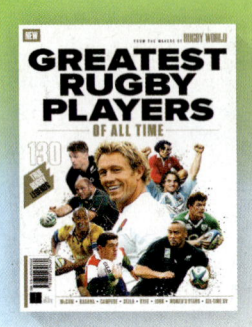

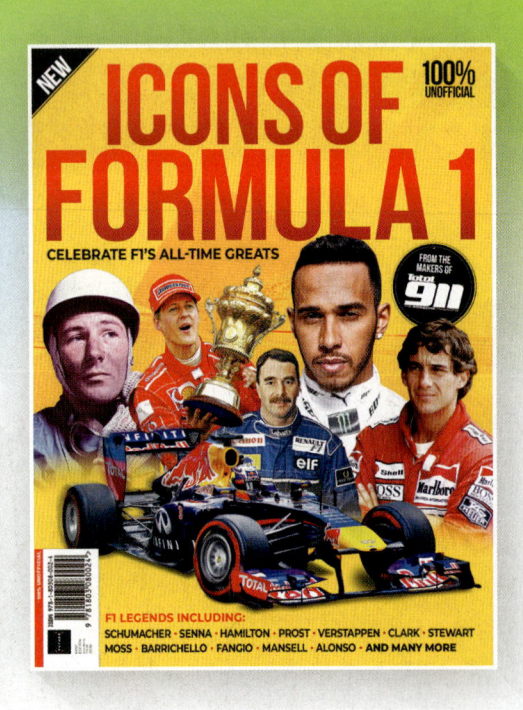

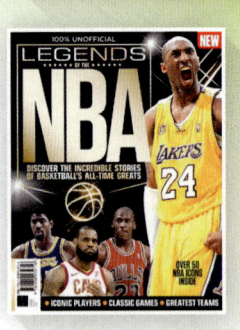

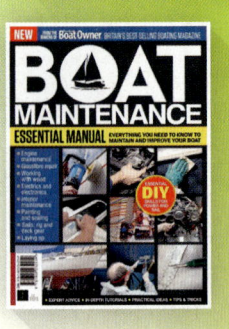

SPORT BOOKAZINES AT THEIR BEST

Whether you're a football fan, golf addict, or love all things F1, we've got you covered with our range of sports titles

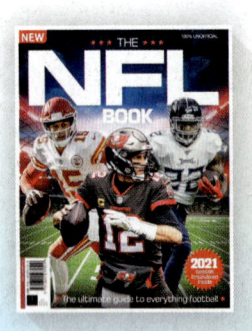

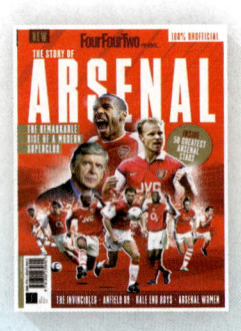

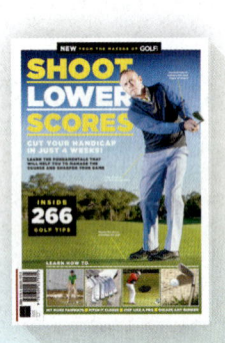

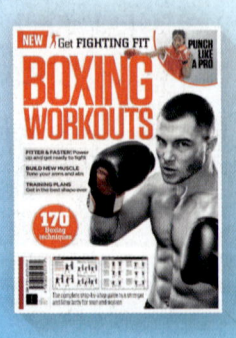

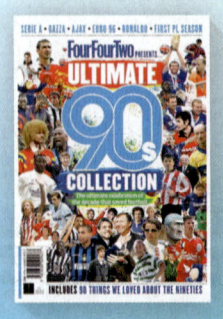

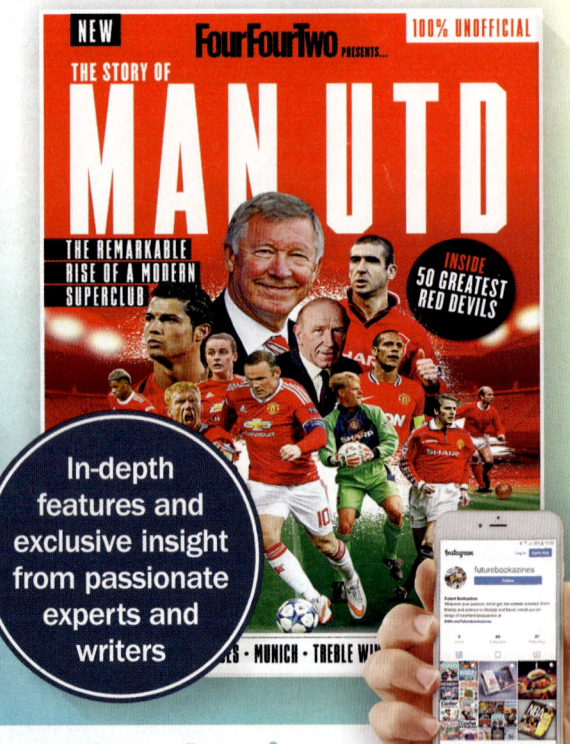

In-depth features and exclusive insight from passionate experts and writers

Follow us on Instagram 📷 @futurebookazines

www.magazinesdirect.com
Magazines, back issues & bookazines.

FUTURE